BASIC GERMAN

Basic German: A Grammar and Workbook comprises an accessible reference grammar and related exercises in a single volume.

The book introduces German people and culture through the medium of the language used today, covering the core material which students would expect to encounter in their first years of learning German.

Each of the 29 units presents one or more related grammar topics, illustrated by examples which serve as models for the exercises that follow. These wide-ranging and varied exercises enable the student to master each grammar point thoroughly.

Features include:

- Clear grammatical explanations with examples in both English and German.
- Authentic language samples from a range of media.
- Checklists at the end of each unit to reinforce key points.
- Cross-referencing to other grammar chapters.
- Full exercise answer key.
- 'Did you know?' sections with extra learning tips on specific grammar points and insights into current usage of German.
- Glossary of grammatical terms.

The new edition has been thoroughly revised, including more varied exercises for practice, and grammar points have been reformulated to use a more learner-centred approach.

Suitable for independent study and for class use, *Basic German: A Grammar and Workbook* is the ideal reference and practice book for beginners, as well as for students with some knowledge of the language.

Heiner Schenke is a principal lecturer in German at the University of Westminster.

Anna Miell is a lecturer in German at the University of Westminster and Trinity Laban Conservatoire of Music and Dance, London.

Karen Seago is the course leader for applied translation at the London Metropolitan University.

Other titles available in the *Grammar Workbooks* series are:

Basic Arabic

Basic Cantonese
Intermediate Cantonese

Basic Chinese
Intermediate Chinese

Basic German
Intermediate German

Basic Irish
Intermediate Irish

Basic Italian

Basic Japanese
Intermediate Japanese

Basic Korean
Intermediate Korean

Basic Latin
Intensive Intermediate Latin

Basic Persian

Basic Polish
Intermediate Polish

Basic Portuguese

Basic Russian
Intermediate Russian

Basic Spanish
Intermediate Spanish

Basic Welsh
Intermediate Welsh

Basic Yiddish

Titles of related interest published by Routledge:

The Routledge Modern German Reader by Maryann Overstreet
German Grammar in Context by Carol Fehringer
Essential German Grammar by Martin Durrell, Katrin Kohl, Gudrun Loftus and Claudia Kaiser
German: An Essential Grammar by Bruce Donaldson

BASIC GERMAN: A GRAMMAR AND WORKBOOK

2nd edition

Heiner Schenke, Anna Miell and Karen Seago

LONDON AND NEW YORK

Second edition published 2016
by Routledge
2 Park Square, Milton Park, Abingdon, Oxon OX14 4RN

and by Routledge
711 Third Avenue, New York, NY 10017

Routledge is an imprint of the Taylor & Francis Group, an informa business

First edition published by Routledge 2003

British Library Cataloguing in Publication Data
A catalogue record for this book is available from the British Library

Library of Congress Cataloging-in-Publication Data
Schenke, Heiner, author.
Basic German : a grammar and workbook / Heiner Schenke, Anna Miell and Karen Seago.— Second Edition.
pages cm
Includes index.
1. German language—Grammar. 2. German language—Textbooks for foreign speakers—English. I. Miell, Anna, author. II. Seago, Karen, author. III. Title.
PF3112.S294 2016
438.2'421—dc23
2015032732

ISBN: 978-1-138-78825-1 (hbk)
ISBN: 978-1-138-78826-8 (pbk)
ISBN: 978-1-315-76568-6 (ebk)

Typeset in Times Ten
by Apex CoVantage, LLC

Printed and bound by CPI Group (UK) Ltd, Croydon, CR0 4YY

CONTENTS

PREFACE

Basic German is aimed at absolute beginners and those learners who have some knowledge of German but who need to refresh and consolidate basic structures. It can be used on its own or in connection with any major German course book, and it is suitable for self-study, class-based learning or reference purposes.

Presentation of grammar

The book explains the essentials of German grammar in clear and simple language. The format is easily accessible, and grammar topics follow a progression which moves from simple aspects to more complex features. For more in-depth study, there are cross-references to related grammar items. Explanations are simple and avoid specialised terminology while introducing key terms. The vocabulary is practical and functional. It is introduced on a cumulative basis and builds on vocabulary associated with topics featured in major course books.

Structure of units

There are 29 units. Each unit covers one key grammar topic, which is contrasted with English structures where appropriate. Each topic starts out with an overview. This is followed by detailed explanation in an easy-to-follow step-by-step layout, breaking down complex aspects into simple segments. Examples in English and German illustrate each point and introduce relevant vocabulary.

Checklists and exercises

Integrated exercises allow immediate practice to consolidate each grammar point. Exercises are varied and progress from simple recognition to more complex application of grammar points.

A checklist at the end of each unit reinforces main points and provides an opportunity to self-assess understanding of the material covered.

Answers to all exercises and checklists are at the end of the book.

Using the book as a grammar reference

Unit headings indicate which grammar point is covered, and the glossary provides clear definitions and simple explanations of key grammatical terms. When appropriate, cross-references are provided within units.

Extra features

Patterns explained

Unit 1 highlights some basic principles where structures of German are fundamentally different from English. It explains their characteristics in simple terms and draws attention to underlying patterns.

'Did you know?' sections

Extra tips on how to learn a language and learning-specific grammar points as well as information on current usage of German are found under the heading 'Did you know?' throughout the book.

The book is suitable for

- independent learners
- GCSE preparation
- AS/A-level revision
- beginners' courses at university and in further education
- adult education courses.

903 8844 Br. City Council Adult Ed 10.06

Stoke Lodge Centre 13-15^{00} Thurs

S9 1BN.

16 sessions from 19 Sep. German Lower Intermediate.

Parking? Space on course? All levels available in daytime

BUT The lower level classes are in morning.

Post-beginners

U 21 Sep - LGB1 Mons: 10-12^{00}: 1B

1C

1D

organiser of lang courses.

Marlis (German) ring me 3 pm Mon today.

Fri am 8 people so far.

1C now, 1D Feb.

2hrs X 16 classes = 32. £198

Fri 20 Sep

spoke first to Sam (office). + Maria

903 8844 Br. City Council Adult Ed 10.06

Stoke Lodge Centre 13-15:00 Thurs

BS9 1BN.

16 sessions from 19 Sep. German courses

Intermediate.

Parking? Free on corner?

post-beginners
Uh 21 Sep - L4B1 Mons: 10-12:00: 1B

1C

1D

Organiser of lang courses. Martin Hope 3 on today. (German)

Sam (office).

All levels available in daytime BUT the lower level classes are in morning.

Fri am 8 people so far.

1C now. 1D Feb.

2 hrs X 16 sessions = 32. £98

Fri 20 Sep

UNIT 1

What's different in German?

Basic tips and patterns

Learning German is often perceived as difficult. In 1880, Mark Twain famously dubbed it 'the awful German language', protesting, 'Surely there is not another language that is so slipshod and systemless, and so slippery and elusive to the grasp' (Mark Twain, 'The awful German language', *The Tramp Abroad*, 1880 (Harmondsworth: Penguin, 1997), pp. 390–402).

But is this really the case? One thing that is very helpful in learning German is that it is a systematic language which follows rules. There are many ways to make these rules easier to learn, and there are quite a few tips which will help you in learning the language.

If you approach the language step by step, you will find that it is much easier than you may think at the beginning. Here are pointers to some basic principles where German is different from English, and which may be useful before you start out with the grammar proper.

Spelling – capital letters and different characters

There are a few ways in which German spelling is different from English.

Capital letters for nouns

German is one of the few languages which uses capital letters not only at the beginning of sentences but also within sentences. In English, this applies only to proper names, to the personal pronoun 'I' and to personifications, such as 'Love'.

In German, all nouns must always be written with a capital letter, regardless of whether they are at the beginning of a sentence or in the middle:

> **Am Wochenende gehen der Mann und die Frau zu einem Yogakurs.**
> At the weekend the man and the woman go to a yoga course.

Note that the pronoun **ich** ('I') has no initial capital in German, but **Sie** (formal form of 'you') does.

Different characters

The German alphabet has some characters which do not exist in the English alphabet:

ß – the sharp 's'

The letter **ß**, called **eszett** in German, is pronounced like the English 's' in 'sun' or 'basic', for example.

German uses this letter, for instance, after **ei** and **ie**, and after **a**, **o** and **u** if they are pronounced long:

heißen	to be called
Straße	street
groß	big

The umlauts – **ä, ö, ü**

These are very important. They change the pronunciation of a word and, more important, its meaning:

Mutter means 'mother', but **M*ü*tter** is the plural form and means 'mothers'.
Musste means 'had to', but **m*ü*sste** means 'should' or 'ought to'.

Three genders

All nouns in German are masculine, feminine or neuter. This shows in their singular article: **der** for masculine, **die** for feminine, **das** for neuter.

It is important to realise that gender in German is grammatical, *not* 'biological' as it is in English. This means that objects, concepts etc. which are neuter ('it') in English can be masculine, feminine or neuter in German:

***der* Tisch**	the table (*masculine*)
***die* Tür**	the door (*feminine*)
***das* Fenster**	the window (*neuter*)

Whenever you learn a new noun, always learn it with its gender: the best way to do this is to learn it with its article. You will find that this will pay off in the long term.

Endings

One of the principal differences between English and German is that, in German, words take specific endings depending on their relationship to other parts of the sentence. This applies to verbs, articles, possessive adjectives and adjectives.

Verbs

These are words describing the 'action' of a sentence, such as 'to run', 'to think'. For example the German verb 'to go' has different endings when used with 'I', 'he' and 'they':

Ich geh*e*.	I go.
Er geh*t*.	He goes.
Sie geh*en*.	They go.

Articles and possessive adjectives

These are words linked to a noun such as 'a', 'the', 'my' or 'his'. For example the indefinite article meaning 'a' changes in German when it is linked to the subject of the sentence (**ein Mann**) or the object of the sentence (**ein*en* Mann**):

Ist das *ein* Mann?	Is that a man?
Da drüben sehe ich ein*en* Mann.	I can see a man over there.

Adjectives

These words, which describe the quality of a noun, such as a 'new' laptop, an 'intelligent' woman or a 'beautiful' house, follow a similar pattern when they appear in front of a noun. In German, adjectives can have different endings when they are linked to a masculine noun (**ein neu*er* Laptop**), a feminine noun (**eine intelligent*e* Frau**) or a neuter noun (**ein schön*es* Haus**).

Cases

One of the most important features of German is that you can tell what function a noun performs in a sentence by the ending of the word that accompanies the noun. That word shows its case. For example a noun can be the subject of the sentence, i.e. the 'agent' of what is happening:

***Der Hund* beißt den Mann.**	*The dog* bites the man.

Or it can be the object, i.e. the 'receiver' of the action in the sentence:

Der Hund beißt *den Mann*.	The dog bites *the man*.

The subject and the object are in different cases, which means that the article ('the') has a different ending. Both 'dog' and 'man' are masculine (**der**), but in the second sentence, 'the dog' is the subject (**der Hund**) and the man is the object (**den Mann**).

Word order

One of the most important features in German word order is the position of the *verb*. In most statements the verb is the *second element*:

Er *hat* zwei Brüder.	He has two brothers.
Morgen *fahre* ich nach Paris.	Tomorrow I'm going to Paris.

However, the verb is at the *beginning* in commands and many questions:

***Öffnen* Sie das Fenster!**	Open the window, please.
***Hast* du ein Tablet?**	Do you have a tablet?

In more complex structures it can also go to the end:

Ich kann morgen nicht kommen, weil ich nach Paris *fahre*.
I can't come tomorrow because I'm going to Paris.

Tenses

English tenses differentiate between an action happening at the moment ('I am working') and an action taking place regularly ('I work at Google'). In German, this difference does not exist. The verb form is the same in both statements:

Ich *arbeite*.	I am working.
Ich *arbeite* bei Google.	I work at Google.

The past in English is expressed either by the *present perfect tense*: 'I have just eaten' or the *simple past tense*: 'I ate'. In the former example, the action reaches into the present, whereas in the latter it finished in the past. In German, however, you use the *present perfect* when you *talk* about the past regardless of when it happened, and you normally use the *simple past* in *written* German.

Words from English

As you may know, German frequently uses words from English, such as **canceln** 'to cancel', **downloaden** 'to download', **lunchen** 'to have lunch', **Meeting** 'meeting' and **Tablet** 'tablet'. However, the meaning or usage can differ from that in English. Throughout the book you'll find plenty of examples that will help you to understand and apply German correctly within a contemporary context.

And finally – looking for principles

German is a very systematic language, and very soon you will realise that there are certain patterns which occur again and again. If you bear this in mind you will see that, after the first few weeks of a fairly steep learning curve, things will become easier and you will recognise these patterns.

Work with a good conventional or online dictionary. It not only gives you a list of translations but also tells you how to pronounce unfamiliar words and gives you important grammatical information, for example whether a verb takes a certain case or what the plural is for a noun. Throughout the book, we tell you how to work with dictionaries to get this kind of information and how it is relevant.

Checklist

1 Where do you use capital letters in German?
2 When do you use the letter **ß**?
3 Why are umlauts important?
4 What is the difference between the use of gender in German and English?
5 What is one of the most important principles affecting German word order?
6 Is there a difference between 'I am working' and 'I work' in German?

1. For all nouns and 'Sie'.
2. ~~For the~~ After a long 's' vowel ~~sound~~ ~~like in 'busy'~~
3. Change the sound and meaning of the word.
4. In English it's biological. In German it's grammatical.
5. Where the verb goes (2nd place normally, 1st place for commands/questions, 3rd place in complex questions.
6. ~~Using 'to'~~ No difference.

UNIT 2
Verbs in the present tense

What is a verb?

A verb usually describes what a person or any other subject in a sentence is *doing*: 'I *go* to the restaurant.' 'She *thinks* about her holiday.' 'They *play* football.' It can also describe a state: 'He *is* angry.' 'She *is* happy.'

Verbs in English

In English, verbs take no endings except for the third person singular ('he'/'she'/'it') in the present tense. You would say: 'I go', 'you go', 'he/she/it go*es*', 'we go', 'you go', 'they go'. Apart from the third person singular, where '-(e)s' is added, the verb appears in the same form as in the *infinitive*, that is the basic form of a verb as it is listed in a dictionary or glossary ('to go').

Verb formation

German has more endings for verbs in the present tense than English does. You take the *stem* of a verb and then add the required ending. The stem is the form of the infinitive without **-en** or **-n**.

infinitive	*stem*	
kommen	**komm**	to come
wohnen	**wohn**	to live
hören	**hör**	to hear

Verb endings – an overview

Here is an overview of the verb endings in the present tense:

		komm-en	*wohn-en*	*hör-en*
ich (I)	**-e**	**komm*e***	**wohn*e***	**hör*e***
du (you, *informal*)	**-st**	**komm*st***	**wohn*st***	**hör*st***

		komm-en	*wohn-en*	*hör-en*
Sie (you, *formal*)	**-en**	**komm*en***	**wohn*en***	**hör*en***
er/sie/es (he/she/it)	**-t**	**komm*t***	**wohn*t***	**hör*t***
wir (we)	**-en**	**komm*en***	**wohn*en***	**hör*en***
ihr (you, *plural, informal*)	**-t**	**komm*t***	**wohn*t***	**hör*t***
Sie (you, *plural, formal*)	**-en**	**komm*en***	**wohn*en***	**hör*en***
sie (they)	**-en**	**komm*en***	**wohn*en***	**hör*en***

A verb with a personal ending as shown above is called a *finite verb*. This is in contrast to the infinitive form of verbs, which mostly ends in **-en**.

Verb endings in more detail

Although as a beginner you may not use all of the verb forms, it is nonetheless important to know them all. Here they are in more detail.

ich ('I')

For the first person singular you add **-e** to the stem:

***Ich* wohn*e* in Frankfurt.**	I live in Frankfurt.
***Ich* spiel*e* Gitarre.**	I play the guitar.

du/Sie ('you', singular)

There are two forms of address in German: the informal and the formal. If you are addressing one person, the informal address is **du** and the formal is **Sie** (always with an initial capital letter). The endings are **-st** and **-en**:

Woher komm*st* du?	Where do you come from? (*informal*)
Wo wohn*st* du?	Where do you live? (*informal*)
Woher komm*en* Sie?	Where do you come from? (*formal*)
Wo wohn*en* Sie?	Where do you live? (*formal*)

er/sie/es ('he', 'she', 'it')

To talk about a third person or an item you use **er** for 'he', **sie** (with small **s**) for 'she' and **es** for 'it' in German and add **-t** to the stem:

***Er* spiel*t* Tennis.**	He plays tennis.
Woher komm*t* *sie*?	Where does she come from?
***Es* funktionier*t*.**	It works.

wir ('we')

Overall the plural forms are much easier to learn. 'We' (**wir**) takes **-en** – the same form as most infinitives:

***Wir* wohn*en* in Köln.**	We live in Cologne.
***Wir* lern*en* Deutsch.**	We learn German.

ihr/Sie ('you', plural)

As for the singular, there is an informal (**ihr**) and a formal way (**Sie**) to address more than one person. These take different endings:

Wo wohn*t ihr*?	Where do you live? (*plural, informal*)
Was mach*t ihr* hier?	What are you doing here? (*plural, informal*)
Wo wohn*en Sie*?	Where do you live? (*plural, formal*)
Was mach*en Sie* hier?	What are you doing here? (*plural, formal*)

sie ('they')

When referring to several people, German uses **sie** again (spelt with a small **s**). You have to add **-en**:

Und woher komm*en sie*?	And where do they come from?
Julia und Tim – was mach*en sie*?	Julia and Tim – what are they doing?

Uses of sie/Sie

When you start learning German you may be confused by the different meanings of the word **sie**.

- **sie** with a small **s** can mean either 'she' or 'they'.
- **Sie** with a capital **S** is used for formal 'you' in both singular and plural.

The verb endings for 'they' and the singular and plural formal 'you' are identical.

One present tense in German

There is only one present tense in German, which corresponds to both the simple and the continuous present tenses in English:

Er trinkt Kaffee.	He drinks coffee. *or* He is drinking coffee.
Sie spielt Fußball.	She plays football. *or* She is playing football.

Exceptions

Although the majority of verbs in German follow the regular pattern described above, there are a number of exceptions (*irregular forms*):

- Some verbs have slight spelling variations, or their stem vowel changes (see Unit 3).
- **Sein** and **haben** ('to be' or 'to have') are particularly irregular (see Unit 4).
- Also modal verbs follow an irregular pattern (see Unit 21).

But before you explore German verb endings further, make sure that you have digested all the information from this unit.

Did you know?

In contemporary German you can find many verbs loaned or adapted from English, such as **joggen** 'to jog', **lunchen** 'to have lunch' and **skypen** 'to skype'. For most of these, you'll apply the usual endings for regular verbs:

Ich jogg*e* jeden Tag.	I go jogging every day.
Sie luncht mit einer Freundin.	She's having lunch with a friend.
Skyp*st* du?	Do you skype?

- For more information on verb endings see Units 3 and 4.
- See also Unit 16 for more details on personal pronouns ('I', 'you', 'he', 'she' etc.).

Exercise 2.1

Use the endings in bold below to complete the table of verb endings below. The first one has been done.

-en -en -e -st -t -en -en -t

ich ***-e***	wir ___
du ___	ihr ___
Sie ___	Sie ___
er/sie/es ___	sie ___

Exercise 2.2

Here is a short interview with Alex Maschke, a student who lives in Berlin. Complete the gaps with the appropriate verb forms.

Example: kommen → Woher ____ du? – Ich ____ aus Frankfurt.
→ Woher ***kommst*** du? – Ich ***komme*** aus Frankfurt.

1 wohnen → Wo ____ du? – Ich ____ jetzt in Berlin.
2 studieren → Und was ____ du? – Ich ____ Physik und Chemie.
3 hören → Welche Musik ____ du? – Ich ____ gern klassische Musik.
4 lernen → Welche Sprache ____ du im Moment? – Ich ____ im Moment Spanisch.
5 trinken → Was ____ du gern? – Ich ____ gern Kaffee.
6 jobben → Und ____ du? – Ja, ich ____ als Kellner in einer Bar.
7 machen → Was ____ du nicht gern? – Ich ____ nicht gern Sport.

As you have probably noticed, Alex was addressed informally. Rewrite the questions in the formal mode (using the **Sie** form).

Example: kommen → Woher ***kommen*** Sie?

Exercise 2.3

Supply the missing endings.

Example: Anna komm__ aus Wien.
→ Anna komm*t* aus Wien.

1 Ich heiß__ Ulrike.
2 Komm__ du wirklich aus London?
3 Peter wohn__ im Stadtzentrum.
4 Das ist Pia. Sie geh__ sehr gern ins Fitnessstudio.
5 Was mach__ dein Bruder?
6 Er studier__ Medizin.
7 Wie heiß__ Sie?
8 Ich heiß__ Petra Schmidt.
9 Und was mach__ Sie beruflich?
10 Ich studier__ Physik.
11 Und woher komm__ ihr?
12 Was mach__ ihr hier?
13 Und wo wohn__ ihr?
14 Wir komm__ aus Süddeutschland.
15 Wir geh__ zu einem Fußballspiel.
16 Wir bleib__ drei Tage.
17 Timo und Sabrina lern__ zusammen Englisch.
18 Basel lieg__ in der Schweiz.
19 Versteh__ ihr Deutsch?
20 Und shopp__ du oft?
21 Jobb__ Ihre Freundin auch?

22 Nein, meine Freundin jobb___ nicht im Moment.
23 Sarah und Tina spiel___ gern Badminton.
24 Wir jogg___ oft im Park und geh___ auch oft schwimmen.

Exercise 2.4

Translate the following sentences.

1 I live in Berlin.
2 He drinks coffee.
3 She plays tennis.
4 We are learning German.
5 Carla and Sophia are playing football.
6 Where do you come from? (Use (*a*) the **du** and (*b*) the **Sie** form.)
7 Where do you live? (Use (*a*) the **du**, (*b*) the **Sie** and (*c*) the **ihr** form.)
8 Do you skype? (Use (*a*) the **du** and (*b*) the **Sie** form.)

Checklist

1 What is the stem of a German verb?
2 Can you name all the verb endings in the singular?
3 Do you know the endings in the plural?
4 How many tenses are there in German for the present?
5 Can you explain what a finite verb is?

UNIT 3

Verb variations and irregular verbs

Regular and irregular forms

Most verbs in German follow a regular pattern where the ending is simply added to the stem of the verb. But there are some variations where the spelling is slightly different. There is also a group of irregular verbs where there are changes in the stem of the verb.

Irregular forms in English

In English, there is also a difference between regular and irregular verbs, but it usually does not affect the present tense, except for 'to be' and 'to have'. These verbs will be discussed in Unit 4.

Spelling variations – an overview

Stems ending in ***-d*** *or* ***-t***

There are some German verbs where the stem ends in **-d** or **-t**. It would be difficult to pronounce the **-st** ending for **du** and the **-t** ending for **er/sie/es** and **ihr** if **-st** or **-t** was added directly to the stem. This is why an **e** is put before these endings:

infinitive	*stem*	*finite verb*	
arbei*t*en	**arbei*t***	**du arbeit*est***	to work
kos*t*en	**kos*t***	**es kost*et***	to cost
re*d*en	**re*d***	**ihr red*et***	to talk

Verbs such as ***atmen*** *and* ***regnen***

Verbs such as **atmen** and **regnen**, where the stem ends in a consonant + **m** or **n**, also need the additional **e**:

infinitive	*stem*	*finite verb*	
a*tm*en	**a*tm***	**du atm*est***	to breathe
reg*n*en	**reg*n***	**es reg*net***	to rain

Examples:

Herr Maier arbeit*et* bei Siemens.	Mr Maier works for Siemens.
Das Ticket kost*et* 5 Euro.	The ticket costs 5 euros.
Ihr red*et* zu viel.	You're talking too much.
Du atm*est* sehr heftig.	You're breathing very heavily.
Es regn*et* schon wieder!	It's raining again!

*Only **du, er/sie/es** and **ihr** forms are affected*

The extra **e** is added only to the endings for the **du**, **er/sie/es** and **ihr** verb forms. The other verb forms are not affected by this:

ich arbeite	**wir arbeiten**
du arbeit*est*	**ihr arbeit*et***
Sie arbeiten	**Sie arbeiten**
er/sie/es arbeit*et*	**sie arbeiten**

*Stems ending in **-s, -ss, -ß, -x** or **-z***

Normally the verb ending for **du** is **-st**, but if the verb stem ends in **-s**, **-ss**, **-ß**, **-x** or **-z** only add a **-t** as the verb ending for **du**.

infinitive	*finite verb*	
reisen	**du rei*st***	to travel
küssen	**du kü*sst***	to kiss
heißen	**du hei*ßt***	to be called
mixen	**du mi*xt***	to mix
tan*z*en	**du tan*zt***	to dance

Examples:

Rei*st* du wieder nach Italien?	Are you travelling to Italy again?
Du hei*ßt* doch Frank, oder?	You're called Frank, aren't you?
Tan*zt* du gern?	Do you like to dance?

*Verbs such as **wandern** and **googeln***

There are some verbs in German whose infinitives don't end in **-en** but in **-ern** or **-eln**. Examples include **wandern** 'to hike', **twittern** 'to tweet', **googeln** 'to google' and **bügeln** 'to iron'. These verbs only add **-n** to the stem of the **Sie**, **wir** and plural **sie** forms:

ich wandere	**wir wander*n***
du wanderst	**ihr wandert**
Sie wander*n*	**Sie wander*n***
er/sie/es wandert	**sie wander*n***

In order to ease pronunciation, verbs ending in **-eln** also drop the letter **e** when used with **ich**:

Ich google alles.	I google everything.
Ich bügle das Hemd.	I am ironing the shirt.

Irregular verbs with vowel changes

There is a group of German verbs where the vowel of the stem changes in the present tense. These changes only apply to the **du** and **er/sie/es** forms. The other verb forms are not affected. Here are some examples:

infinitive	*finite verb*	
schlafen	**du schl*ä*fst**	to sleep
essen	**du *i*sst**	to eat
sprechen	**er spr*i*cht**	to speak
lesen	**er l*ie*st**	to read
sehen	**sie s*ie*ht**	to see

Examples:

L*ie*st du gern E-Books?	Do you like reading e-books?
Er s*ie*ht ein Baseballmatch.	He is watching a baseball match.
Sie *i*sst gern Pizza.	She likes eating pizza.
Spr*i*chst du Deutsch?	Do you speak German?
Sie schl*ä*ft bis elf Uhr.	She sleeps until eleven o'clock.

Looking out for patterns

These vowel changes apply only to a limited number of verbs. It is best to learn these verbs by heart. There are also certain patterns which can help you predict how a verb changes. They are:

a → ä

e → i

e → ie

Here they are in more detail.

*Changes from **a** to **ä***

Important verbs – apart from **schlafen** – which follow this pattern are:

f*a*hren	→	**du f*ä*hrst, er/sie/es f*ä*hrt**	to drive
f*a*llen		**du f*ä*llst, er/sie/es f*ä*llt**	to fall
tr*a*gen		**du tr*ä*gst, er/sie/es tr*ä*gt**	to carry
w*a*schen		**du w*ä*schst, er/sie/es w*ä*scht**	to wash

Examples:

Du f*ä*hrst morgen nach Hause.	You're going home tomorrow.
Gleich f*ä*llt es runter!	Any moment now it will fall (down)!
Er tr*ä*gt ein neues T-Shirt.	He wears a new T-shirt.

*Changes from **e** to **i***

The verbs **sprechen** and **essen** are two frequently used verbs which change their stem vowel from **e** to **i**. Other verbs which follow this pattern are:

geben	→	**du g*i*bst, er/sie/es g*i*bt**	to give
helfen		**du h*i*lfst, er/sie/es h*i*lft**	to help
treffen		**du tr*i*ffst, er/sie/es tr*i*fft**	to meet
werfen		**du w*i*rfst, er/sie/es w*i*rft**	to throw

Examples:

Er h*i*lft Frau Maier.	He helps Frau Maier.
Tr*i*ffst du heute Sofia?	Are you meeting Sofia today?
Sie w*i*rft den Ball zu Max.	She throws the ball to Max.

The verb **nehmen** 'to take' also follows the **e** to **i** pattern, but it has additional spelling variations. Here are all forms:

ich nehme	**wir nehmen**
du n*imm*st	**ihr nehmt**
Sie nehmen	**Sie nehmen**
er/sie/es n*imm*t	**sie nehmen**

Examples:

N*imm*st du die U-Bahn?	Are you taking the underground/subway?
Er n*imm*t ein Bad.	He is having a bath.

*Changes from **e** to **ie***

Some verbs such as **sehen** and **lesen**, where the **e** sound is pronounced long, the main **e** sound into **ie**:

s*e*hen	→	**du s*ie*hst, er/sie/es s*ie*ht**	to see
l*e*sen		**du l*ie*st, er/sie/es l*ie*st**	to read

Another important verb is **empfehlen**:

empf*e*hlen	→	**du empf*ie*hlst, er/sie/es empf*ie*hlt**	to recommend

Examples:

Er s*ie*ht Mira nicht.	He doesn't see Mira.
Was empf*ie*hlst du?	What do you recommend?

Where to look for irregular forms

All verbs with a vowel change are irregular verbs. You will find a list of irregular verbs, often also called strong verbs, in most course books, conventional or online dictionaries, as well as here on page (page 210). But please note – not all irregular verbs change their spelling in the present tense.

Other irregular verbs

There are also two other groups of verb forms which do not conform to the regular pattern in the present tense:

- the verbs **sein** 'to be' and **haben** 'to have' (see Unit 4)
- the modal verbs (see Unit 21).

Did you know?

In Switzerland the letter **ß** has been abandoned and is normally replaced with **ss**. **Straße** becomes **Strasse**, and **heißen** is spelt **heissen**. Its present tense forms are **ich heisse**, **du heisst**, **Sie heissen**, **er/sie/es heisst**, **wir heissen**, **ihr heisst**, **Sie heissen**, **sie heissen**.

Exercise 3.1

Write out the full present tense of the following verbs (for all persons: **ich**, **du**, **Sie**, **er/sie/es**, **wir**, **ihr**, **Sie**, **sie**):

1 arbeiten
2 tanzen
3 heißen
4 reisen
5 googeln

Exercise 3.2

Below is a list of frequently used irregular verbs. Place a tick next to the ones which change their vowel in the present tense and a cross next to the ones which do not. The first two have been done. Use a verb list, e.g. the one on page 210, to check your answers.

bleiben	×	*helfen*		*schreiben*		*stehen*	
essen	✓	kommen		schwimmen		tragen	
fahren		nehmen		sehen		treffen	
geben		lesen		singen		trinken	
gehen		schlafen		sprechen		waschen	

Exercise 3.3

Here is what Hans Homann, a young radio presenter from Austria, says about himself. Use this information to write a short portrait of him. The first sentence has been done for you.

1 Ich heiße Hans Homann. → Er heißt Hans Homann.
2 Ich komme aus Wien.
3 Ich arbeite bei Radio Ö24.
4 Ich esse zu Mittag meistens Sushi.
5 Ich spreche natürlich Deutsch, aber auch Englisch und Spanisch.
6 Ich lese gern Kriminalromane.
7 Ich fahre auch gern Ski und schwimme viel.
8 Ich sehe gern Filme mit Michael Keaton.
9 Ich schlafe oft lange.

10 Ich reise gern.
11 Am Abend treffe ich oft Freunde im Kaffeehaus.
12 Am Wochenende helfe ich manchmal alten Leuten.

Exercise 3.4

Translate the following sentences into German.

1 She reads a book.
2 Peter speaks German and English.
3 We speak German and Spanish.
4 Magda likes eating pizza.
5 I am meeting Nadine.
6 She is taking the underground.
7 He is wearing a T-shirt.
8 It is raining.

Checklist

1 Do you know what happens to a verb when its stem ends in a **-d** or **-t**?
2 What do you have to be aware of with verbs such as **googeln** and **bügeln**?
3 Which verb forms are affected by a stem vowel change?
4 Can you name three frequently used verbs that change their stem vowel from **e** to **i**?

UNIT 4

Irregular verbs: **haben** and **sein**

Irregular in both languages

The verbs **haben** 'to have' and **sein** 'to be' are both very important. They are quite irregular in German, as in English.

Different patterns

As explained in Unit 3, irregular verbs in German tend to change their stem vowel. In the present tense this sometimes affects the **du** and **er/sie/es** forms:

lesen	→	**du l*ie*st, er/sie/es l*ie*st**	to read
essen		**du *i*sst, er/sie/es *i*sst**	to eat

Sein is an example of an irregular verb whose forms change even more drastically. This is very similar to English, where 'to be' has very irregular forms in the present tense: 'I am', 'you are', 'he/she/it is', 'we are', 'you are', 'they are'.

Haben *and* ***sein*** *– an overview*

Here is an overview of the verb forms for **haben** and **sein**:

	haben	*sein*
ich (I)	**habe**	**bin**
du (you, *informal*)	**hast**	**bist**
Sie (you, *formal*)	**haben**	**sind**
er/sie/es (he/she/it)	**hat**	**ist**
wir (we)	**haben**	**sind**
ihr (you, *plural, informal*)	**habt**	**seid**
Sie (you, *plural, formal*)	**haben**	**sind**
sie (they)	**haben**	**sind**

Here are both verbs in more detail.

Haben in more detail

Different patterns for **du** *and* **er/sie/es**

There are some patterns with **haben** which may help you remember the endings.

The endings for **ich**, **Sie**, **wir**, **ihr**, **Sie** and **sie** ('they') are regular: you add them to the stem in the normal way: **ich hab-e**, **Sie hab-en**, **wir hab-en**, **ihr hab-t**, **Sie hab-en**, **sie hab-en**.

It is only for **du** and **er/sie/es** that the verb form is irregular – you need to drop the **b** from the stem: **du hast**, **er/sie/es hat**.

Examples:

Ich habe viel zu tun.	I have a lot to do.
Hast du Wechselgeld?	Have you got any change?
Claus hat eine Schwester.	Claus has a sister.
Sie haben ein neues Auto.	They have a new car.

Use of **haben**

Haben is an important verb which you will be using a lot. It is used on its own but also with other verbs as a so-called auxiliary verb, where it helps to form other structures, for instance the present perfect tense:

Ich habe viel gesungen.	I have sung a lot.

Useful phrases

Here are a few useful phrases with **haben**:

Hunger haben	to be hungry	**Ich habe Hunger.**
Durst haben	to be thirsty	**Er hat Durst.**
Zeit haben	to be free/have time	**Du hast Zeit.**
Glück haben	to be lucky	**Sie haben Glück.**
Langeweile haben	to be bored	**Wir haben Langeweile.**
Kopfschmerzen haben	to have a headache	**Sie hat Kopfschmerzen.**

Sein in more detail

Completely irregular

The verb forms for **sein** are completely irregular and are best learned by heart: **ich bin**, **du bist**, **Sie sind**, **er/sie/es ist**, **wir sind**, **ihr seid**, **Sie sind**, **sie sind**.

Examples:

Ich bin aus Deutschland.	I'm from Germany.
Du bist sehr schön.	You're very beautiful.
Sind Sie Herr Diez?	Are you Mr Diez?
Er ist Amerikaner.	He is an American.
Sie ist Lehrerin.	She is a teacher.
Es ist schwer.	It's difficult.
Wir sind beide 20 Jahre alt.	We are both 20 years old.
Seid ihr verheiratet?	Are you married?
Wir sind aus Großbritannien.	We're from Great Britain.

*Use of **sein***

Like **haben**, **sein** has an important role in German and can be used on its own and also as an auxiliary verb in connection with other verbs, for instance the present perfect tense (see Unit 22).

Reminder – only one present tense in German

Although there are many similarities between the use of 'to be' and **sein** in English and German, there are also important differences. You cannot, for instance, use **sein** to form a structure such as 'I am going' in English. This tense does not exist in German. There is only one present tense: **Ich gehe**.

Did you know?

'To be or not to be, that is the question', is one of the best-known quotes by William Shakespeare. His play *Hamlet*, among his other works, is regularly performed in German. In the translation, 'to be' turns into **sein** and the complete quote becomes: **Sein oder Nichtsein, das ist hier die Frage.**

- For more irregular verb endings in the present tense see Unit 3.
- To remind yourself of the regular endings see Unit 2.

Exercise 4.1

Complete the following sentences with the correct verb forms of **haben**.

Example: Ich ____ eine Schwester.
→ Ich ***habe*** eine Schwester.

1 ____ du heute Abend Zeit?
2 Wir ____ neue Nachbarn.

3 Er ____ eine Schwester und einen Bruder.
4 ____ ihr etwas Geld?
5 Nadine ____ ein neues Tablet.
6 ____ Sie ein Zimmer frei?
7 Ich ____ Hunger.
8 Susanne und Frank ____ eine neue Wohnung.

Exercise 4.2

Use the appropriate verb forms of **sein** to complete the following short dialogues.

Example: Was ____ Carsten von Beruf? – Er ____ Student.
→ Was ***ist*** Carsten von Beruf? – Er ***ist*** Student.

1 ____ Sie Engländer?	– Nein, ich ____ aus Australien.
2 ____ du aus Deutschland?	– Ja, ich komme aus der Nähe von Bonn.
3 ____ ihr aus München?	– Nein, wir ____ aus Nürnberg.
4 Was ____ Nele von Beruf?	– Sie ____ Designerin.
5 Was machen Katrin und Jan?	– Beide ____ Studenten.
6 Was ____ deine Hobbys?	– Mein Hobbys ____ Musik und Computerspiele.
7 Wo ____du geboren?	– Ich ____ in Düsseldorf geboren.
8 Wo ____ ihr geboren?	– Wir ____ beide in den USA geboren.

Exercise 4.3

Now write out the full present tense (for all persons: **ich**, **du**, **Sie**, **er/sie/es**, **wir**, **ihr**, **Sie**, **sie**) of the verbs (1) **haben** and (2) **sein**.

Exercise 4.4

Translate the following sentences into German.

1 We are from New York.
2 They are from Australia.
3 Mario is from Munich.
4 Are you Mr Becker? (Use the **Sie** form.)
5 He has a sister.
6 Do you have time? (Use (*a*) the **du** and (*b*) the **Sie** form.)
7 They are students.
8 I have a tablet.
9 It's difficult.
10 Bonn is in Germany and Salzburg is in Austria.

Checklist

1 Do you know all the verb forms (in the present tense) for **sein**?
2 Which are the two irregular forms of **haben**?
3 Can you remember some useful phrases with **haben**?
4 Can you say 'To be or not to be' in German?

UNIT 5
Separable verbs in the present tense

What is a separable verb?

These are verbs which are made up of two parts: a *prefix* and a *main verb*. For example **auf** + **stehen** → **aufstehen** 'to get up'.

Comparison with English

Separable verbs are formed in a similar way to English phrasal verbs, which consist of a main verb plus an adverb or preposition: 'to get up', 'to get on' etc.

Important separable verbs

Separable verbs are quite frequent in German. Here are some of the most important ones:

abfahren	to leave, to depart
abholen	to pick up, to collect
abwaschen	to do the washing up
anfangen	to start
ankommen	to arrive
anrufen	to phone
aufhören	to stop
aufräumen	to tidy up
aufstehen	to get up
ausgehen	to go out
ausschalten	to switch off
einkaufen	to go shopping
einladen	to invite
einschlafen	to fall asleep
fernsehen	to watch television
mitbringen	to bring along
mitkommen	to come along

mitmachen	to join in
stattfinden	to take place
vorbereiten	to prepare
sich vorstellen	to introduce oneself
zumachen	to close

Prefixes go at the end

When a separable verb is in the present tense, the prefix is usually separated from the main part of the verb and goes to the end of the sentence:

anrufen	→	**Herr Lobo *ruft* seine Frau *an*.** Mr Lobo rings his wife.
aufstehen		**Nico *steht* um fünf Uhr morgens *auf*.** Nico gets up at five o'clock in the morning.
ausgehen		**Yasmin *geht* jeden Tag *aus*.** Yasmin goes out every day.
fernsehen		**Die Kinder *sehen* nicht viel *fern*.** The children don't watch much television.
einkaufen		**Er *kauft* im Supermarkt *ein*.** He goes shopping in the supermarket.
stattfinden		**Das Meeting *findet* am Montag *statt*.** The meeting takes place on Monday.

Separable verbs in two clauses

When a sentence consists of two main clauses, the split-off prefix goes to the end of the relevant clause. This may not necessarily be at the end of the sentence.

clause 1	*clause 2*	
Ich *stehe auf*	**und dann frühstücke ich.**	I get up and then I have breakfast.
Herr Carlsen *sieht fern*,	**aber seine Kinder lesen.**	Mr Carlsen is watching television, but his children are reading.

If you have a sentence with two main clauses which use separable verbs, then you have the split-off part at the end of each clause:

Herr Schuster *schläft* erst um Mitternacht *ein*, aber er *steht* schon um fünf Uhr *auf*.

Mr Schuster only falls asleep at midnight, but he gets up at five o'clock.

Verbs can have more than one prefix

A verb can be combined with more than one prefix. Here are examples of the different meanings that the verb **machen** 'to make' has when joined up with various prefixes:

***an*machen**	to turn/switch on
***auf*machen**	to open
***aus*machen**	to turn/switch off
***mit*machen**	to join in
***nach*machen**	to imitate
***sauber*machen**	to clean
***weiter*machen**	to continue
***zu*machen**	to close

Another example is the verb **kommen**: ***an*kommen** means to 'arrive', ***heraus*kommen** 'to come out', ***mit*kommen** 'to come along' and ***zurück*kommen** 'to come back, to return '.

You can quite often guess the meaning by knowing what the prefix means. But that does not work all the time, so meanings of separable verbs need to be learned.

How to find out whether a verb is separable

You can find out whether a verb is separable by checking in a good conventional dictionary. After the main entry in the German-English section, it will say '*sep*' if it is separable. In online dictionaries separable verbs are not always identified.

Common separable prefixes

The most common separable prefixes are:

ab-, **an-**, **auf-**, **aus-**, **ein-**, **mit-**, **nach-**, **vor-**, **zu-**, **zurück-**

You will find examples of most of these prefixes used with a verb in the preceding pages.

Some inseparable prefixes

There are also prefixes which cannot be detached from the verb. They include **be-**, **er-**, **ge-** and **ver-**. Frequently used verbs with inseparable prefixes are **bezahlen** 'to pay', **erzählen** 'to tell', **gewinnen** 'to win', **verkaufen** 'to sell' and **verstehen** 'to understand'.

Er *be*zahlt mit seiner Kreditkarte. He pays with his credit card.
Sie *ver*kauft ihren alten Laptop. She is selling her old laptop.

Verbs with an inseparable prefix are called inseparable verbs.

More about separable verbs

If you cannot find a separable verb in a verb list and want to find out whether it is regular or irregular, just look up the main part of the separable verb. So, for example, to find out the verb forms of **abfahren**, look up **fahren**.

As a beginner you will probably use separable verbs most often as explained above. However, separable verbs also occur in other structures:

- with the imperative (Unit 6);
- in combination with modal verbs (Unit 21);
- in various tenses (Units 22–24);
- with subordinate clauses (Units 28–29).

Did you know?

Separable verbs are often used with language connected to technology and modern media. Examples include **anhängen** 'to attach', **ausdrucken** 'to print out', **hochladen** 'to upload' and **herunterladen** 'to download':

Ich hänge die Datei an. I attach the file.
Wir drucken den Artikel aus. We'll print out the article.
Wer lädt das Video hoch? Who's uploading the video?
Er lädt die Fotos herunter. He is downloading the photos.

Exercise 5.1

Here is a description of Jens Fischer's day. Complete the gaps with the finite verb and the prefix.

Example: Jens ____ den Wecker um sieben Uhr ____. (ausschalten)
→ Jens ***schaltet*** den Wecker um sieben Uhr ***aus***.

1 Jens ____ um halb acht Uhr ____. (aufstehen)
2 Er ____ seine Arbeit um neun Uhr ____. (anfangen)
3 Mittags ____ er seine Freundin ____. (anrufen)
4 Er ____ am Nachmittag viele Dokumente ____. (ausdrucken)
5 Um siebzehn Uhr ____ er mit seiner Arbeit ____. (aufhören)

6 Nach der Arbeit ____ er im Supermarkt ____. (einkaufen)
7 Abends ____ er manchmal ____. (fernsehen)
8 Am Wochenende ____ er oft ____. (ausgehen)
9 Er ____ meistens ____ nach Mitternacht ____. (einschlafen)

Three of the verbs from the exercise require a vowel change. Do you know which ones?

Exercise 5.2

Which of the following verbs are separable? Put a tick next to them. The first separable verb has been done. If you are not sure, check in a dictionary.

aufstehen	✓	verlieren		abfahren		anrufen	
verkaufen		fernsehen		anhängen		stattfinden	
einladen		mitkommen		bezahlen		erzählen	
aufräumen		frühstücken		einkaufen		besuchen	

Exercise 5.3

Now use the separable verbs from Exercise 5.2 to fill in the gaps below. The first one has been done.

1 Herr und Frau Nowitzki ***stehen*** um sieben Uhr ***auf***.
2 Die Kinder ____ ihr Zimmer ____.
3 Er ____ immer im Supermarkt ____.
4 Wir gehen ins Café. ____ du ____ ?
5 Wann ____ das Konzert ____ ?
6 Herr Beckmann liebt TV-Serien. Er ____ jeden Tag ____.
7 Wann ____ der nächste Zug nach Hamburg ____ ?
8 Wir ____ viele Gäste zu unserer Party ____.
9 Philip ____ eine Datei ____.
10 Sie hat ein neues Smartphone und ____ ihre Freundin ____.

Exercise 5.4

Translate the following sentences.

1 I get up at six o'clock.
2 I start my work at eight o'clock.
3 The meeting takes place on Monday.

4 When does the train leave?
5 When does the train arrive?
6 The children are watching television.
7 Are you coming along?
8 I attach the file and print out the article.

Checklist

1 Which part of a separable verb is split off?
2 Where does the split-off part normally go in a sentence?
3 Can you name a few separable prefixes?
4 How can you check in a conventional dictionary whether a verb is separable?
5 Do you know three prefixes which are non-separable?

UNIT 6
Imperatives

What is the imperative?

The imperative is used for making requests or instructing people to do things.

The imperative in English

In English, the imperative works by using the verb form of the infinitive:

Close the window! *Switch off* your mobile! *Be* happy!

Whether you are addressing only one person or several, there is no change.

Different forms in German

The imperative in German is a bit more complicated. There are different forms, depending on whether you are addressing one person only or more than one. German also distinguishes between the formal and informal mode of address in the imperative.

Imperatives – an overview

Here is an overview of the different forms of the imperative:

	singular		*plural*	
	du	*Sie*	*ihr*	*Sie*
kommen	**Komm!**	**Kommen Sie!**	**Kommt!**	**Kommen Sie!**
warten	**Warte!**	**Warten Sie!**	**Wartet!**	**Warten Sie!**
sprechen	**Sprich leise!**	**Sprechen Sie leise!**	**Sprecht leise!**	**Sprechen Sie leise!**

	singular		*plural*	
	du	*Sie*	*ihr*	*Sie*
anfangen	**Fang an!**	**Fangen Sie an!**	**Fangt an!**	**Fangen Sie an!**
haben	**Hab Geduld.**	**Haben Sie Geduld.**	**Habt Geduld.**	**Haben Sie Geduld.**
sein	**Sei vorsichtig.**	**Seien Sie vorsichtig.**	**Seid vorsichtig.**	**Seien Sie vorsichtig.**

As you can see, the **du**, **Sie** and **ihr** forms follow different patterns. The imperative with **Sie** is the same in the singular and plural.

Imperatives in more detail

Here are the different forms in more detail.

*Addressing one person informally (**du** form)*

The *informal singular* **du** form is used with one person with whom you are quite familiar – children, family or friends.

Formation

You form the imperative by using the stem of the verb without an ending:

komm-en	→	**komm**	**Komm her!**	Come (here)!
trink-en		**trink**	**Trink weniger.**	Drink less.

Irregular forms

Verbs which have some variations in their present tense also have slight variations for the imperative:

- Verbs whose stem ends in **-d**, **-t**, consonant + **m** or consonant + **n** add **-e**.

warten	→	**wart** (+ **-e**)	**Warte!**	Wait!
öffnen		**öffn** (+ **-e**)	**Öffne die Tür.**	Open the door.

- Verbs which have a *stem vowel change* have the same stem vowel change in the imperative:

sprechen	→	**sprich**	**Sprich leise!**	Talk quietly.
lesen		**lies**	**Lies die SMS.**	Read the text message.

- But verbs which have a *stem vowel change* from **a** to **ä** do *not* change. They simply use the stem to form the imperative:

fahren	→	**fahr**	**Fahr rechts!**	Drive on the right!
tragen		**trag**	**Trag das rote Kleid.**	Wear the red dress.

Separable verbs

Separable verbs split off their prefix and place it after the verb or at the end of the clause:

anfangen	→	**fang … an**	**Fang an!**	Start!
mitmachen		**mach . . . mit**	**Mach bitte mit.**	Join in, please.

Haben and **sein**

Haben and **sein** behave like regular verbs. Their forms derive from the verb stem:

hab-en	→	**hab**	**Hab Geduld.**	Be patient.
sei-n		**sei**	**Sei vorsichtig.**	Be careful.

*Addressing one person formally (**Sie** form)*

If you address one person you are not familiar with, use the *formal singular* **Sie** form.

Formation

Simply use the verb form of the infinitive. Unlike the **du** form, the formal imperative uses the personal pronoun **Sie**. You can tell that it is an imperative because the **Sie** comes *after* the verb:

kommen	→	**Kommen Sie, bitte.**	Please come.
warten		**Warten Sie!**	Wait!

Separable verbs

Separable verbs split as before:

anfangen	→	**Fangen Sie bitte an.**	Please start.

Haben and **sein**

For **haben** just use the infinitive, but for **sein** you'll need to add an extra **e**:

haben	→	**Haben Sie Geduld.**	Be patient.
sein		**Sei*e*n Sie vorsichtig.**	Be careful.

*Addressing more than one person informally (**ihr** form)*

The informal plural is used when you are addressing two or more people you are familiar with – children, family or friends.

Formation

In the imperative there is no change to the usual formation of the second person plural (**ihr**): simply add **t** to the stem of the verb. This also includes **haben**. Note the following points:

- Verbs which take an *additional* **e** because their stem ends in **-d**, **-t**, consonant + **m** or consonant + **n** also have the ending stem -**et**.
- The verb **sein** is an exception and is spelt **seid**.
- *Separable verbs* split off their prefix.

kommen	→	**Komm*t*, bitte!**	Please come!
warten		**Wart*et* auf uns!**	Wait for us!
sein		**Seid freundlich.**	Be friendly.
aufhören		**Hör*t* mit dem Reden *auf*.**	Stop talking.

*Addressing more than one person formally (**Sie** form)*

If you address more than one person in a formal way, you use the **Sie** plural form. As the formal imperative does not differentiate between singular and plural, it is formed exactly like the singular:

kommen	→	**Kommen Sie, meine Herren.**	Gentlemen, please come.
sein		**Seien Sie pünktlich.**	Be punctual.
warten		**Warten Sie!**	Wait!
eintreten		**Bitte treten Sie ein.**	Please enter.

Verb in first position

As you have seen, all imperative forms in German have one important feature in common: the verb is placed in the first position in the sentence. This structure is very similar to English.

Exclamation marks

In written German, you often put an exclamation mark after the command form. This puts more emphasis on what is being said.

Did you know?

The imperative is used quite frequently in German. It is normally not being perceived as being impolite or rude, especially when used with **bitte** 'please'.

English tends to use more elaborate structures, often in question form: 'Could you open the window, please?' Although Germans quite often use similar phrases, be prepared for the imperative as well.

Exercise 6.1

Complete these requests and commands by using the verbs in brackets.

Example: ______ Sie langsamer, bitte. (reden)
→ ***Reden*** Sie langsamer, bitte.

1 ______ Sie mir noch einen Saft, bitte. (bringen)
2 ______ Sie bitte das Fenster. (öffnen)
3 ______ Sie bitte noch fünf Minuten. (warten)
4 ______ Sie mir eine SMS. (schicken)
5 ______ Sie ____ ! (hereinkommen)
6 ______ Sie ____ ! (anfangen)
7 ______ Sie bitte ruhig. (sein)
8 ______ Sie ein bisschen Geduld. (haben)

Exercise 6.2

Now rewrite the sentences from Exercise 6.1, this time using the **du** form.

Example: ***Rede*** langsamer, bitte.

Exercise 6.3

You are telling a close friend how she could improve her health. Put the following in the imperative using the **du** form.

Example: mehr Zeit für sich selber / haben
→ Hab mehr Zeit für dich selber!

1 mehr mit dem Fahrrad / fahren
2 zu einem Yogakurs / gehen
3 weniger / fernsehen
4 mehr Gemüse / essen
5 einen Blog über Gesundheit / lesen
6 mehr / schlafen
7 relaxter / sein
8 mehr / ausgehen
9 eine bessere Work-Life-Balance / finden

Exercise 6.4

Translate the following sentences. Use first the **Sie** form, then the **du** form and finally the **ihr** form.

1 Please start.
2 Open the window.
3 Send me a text message.
4 Be careful.

Checklist

1 Can you name the different imperative forms in German?
2 How do you form the singular informal imperative?
3 Which verb variations also apply in the formation of the imperative?
4 How do you recognise the formal imperative?

UNIT 7
Questions

Two types of questions

There are two main types of questions. The first, often called a *wh-question*, starts with a question word (*interrogative*) and tends to be more 'open'. The second starts with a verb and requires 'yes' or 'no' as an answer.

Similar use in English and German

Both types are frequently used in English and German:

Wh-question

Where do you come from?	**Woher kommen Sie?**
Where do you live?	**Wo wohnen Sie?**

Yes or no question

Have you got brothers and sisters?	**Haben Sie Geschwister?**
Is this your mobile?	**Ist das Ihr Handy?**

Here are both types in more detail.

Wh-questions in detail

Frequently used question words

Here is a list of important question words and their English equivalents:

wer?	who?
was?	what?

wo?	where?
woher?	where ... from?
wohin?	where ... (to)?
wann?	when?
wie?	how? what?
wie lange?	how long?
wie viel?	how much?
wie viele?	how many?
wie oft?	how often?
warum?	why?

Here are some examples which show how the question words work:

Wer ist das?	Who is that?
Wo wohnst du?	Where do you live?
Woher kommen Sie?	Where do you come from?
Wohin fährt Juliane nächstes Wochenende?	Where is Juliane going next weekend?
Wie ist deine E-Mail-Adresse?	What is your email address?
Wie viel kostet das I-Pad?	How much is the iPad?
Wie oft gehst du aus?	How often do you go out?
Was sind Ihre Hobbys?	What are your hobbies?

Useful points

As you can see, the usage of most question words in German is very similar to that in English. Note the following points.

Use of ***wie*** *for names and addresses*

The German question word **wie** 'how' is also used when you ask for a name, number, address or time:

Wie ist dein Name?	What is your name?
Wie ist Ihre Handynummer/Adresse?	What is your mobile number/address?
Wie viel Uhr ist es?	What's the time?

It is incorrect to use **was** in such questions.

Use of ***wo, wohin*** *and* ***woher***

Note that **wo** corresponds to the English 'where'. If motion to or from a place is indicated, German uses **wohin** and **woher**:

Wo ist die Kirche?	Where is the church?
Wohin gehst du heute Abend?	Where are you going (to) this evening?
Woher kommst du gerade?	Where have you just come from?

How to ask about professions and where you work

The most common way in German to ask what somebody does for a living is:

Was sind Sie von Beruf?	What do you do for a living? *lit.* What are you by profession?

To find out where somebody is working, the question in German is:

Wo arbeiten Sie?	Where do you work?

Question words in first position

The question word occupies the first place in a question. It is followed by the verb as the second element and then the subject:

question word	*verb*	*subject*	*other elements*
Woher	**kommen**	**Sie?**	
Wohin	**fährt**	**Juliane**	**am Wochenende?**

Yes or no questions in detail

Formation

The second type of question can be answered by a simple 'yes' or 'no'. As you can see, it does not need a question word. Instead, the verb moves into the first position:

finite verb	*subject*	*other elements*
Skypst	**du**	**gern?**
Wohnen	**Sie**	**im Hotel ‚Zur Sonne'?**
Kommt	**Peter**	**aus Berlin?**

This structure differs from a statement, where the verb is the second element:

statement	*question*
Sie *wohnen* im Hotel ‚Zur Sonne'.	***Wohnen* Sie im Hotel ‚Zur Sonne'?**
Peter *kommt* aus Berlin.	***Kommt* Peter aus Berlin?**

Simpler structure than English

English often uses the verb 'to do' to form this kind of question: 'Do you like to skype?' 'Do you stay in the hotel "Zur Sonne"?' 'Does Peter come from Berlin?'

In German, these kind of structure does not exist. It is sufficient to move the verb to the beginning of the sentence. Here are some more examples:

Sprechen Sie Deutsch?	Do you speak German?
Arbeitet er bei Hugo Boss?	Does he work for Hugo Boss?
Fährt der Zug um acht Uhr ab?	Does the train depart at eight o'clock?

Did you know?

If you are surprised by something you hear and would like to verify it, you can add **wirklich** 'really' in German to put more emphasis on your question:

Kommt Timo *wirklich* aus Bremen?	Does Timo *really* come from Bremen?
Ist das *wirklich* wahr?	Is this *really* true?
Liegt Genf *wirklich* in der Schweiz?	Is Geneva *really* in Switzerland?

Exercise 7.1

Supply the missing question words from the list. The first one has been done.

wo ~~wie~~ wie wann wo was wie wie woher wie woher wohin

1 ***Wie*** heißen Sie?
2 ____ wohnen Sie?
3 ____ ist Ihre E-Mail-Adresse?
4 ____ arbeiten Sie?
5 ____ sind Sie von Beruf?
6 ____ kommen Sie eigentlich?
7 ____ viel kostet das?
8 ____ beginnt der Workshop?
9 ____ viel Uhr ist es?
10 ____ kommt der Tennisspieler?
11 ____ fahren wir am Sonntag?
12 ____ viele Einwohner hat Deutschland?

Exercise 7.2

You are somewhat surprised by the information given in these statements. Query them by asking *yes or no questions*, using **wirklich** to emphasise your point.

Example: Jana spricht sehr gut Englisch.
→ Spricht Jana wirklich sehr gut Englisch?

1 Das Restaurant ist sehr billig.
2 Leon ist verheiratet.
3 Frau Weber macht viel Sport.
4 Das Smartphone kostet nur 80 Euro.
5 Jennifer und Max stehen um sechs Uhr auf.

Exercise 7.3

Here is an interview with Oliver Gehrs, who is a well-known journalist. Can you figure out what the questions were?

Example: *Wie alt sind Sie*?
– Ich bin 32 Jahre alt.

1 ____________________________?
– Mein Name ist Oliver Gehrs.
2 ____________________________?
– Ich bin Journalist.
3 ____________________________?
– Meine Arbeit beginnt meistens um 8.00 Uhr.
4 ____________________________?
– Ja, die Arbeit ist sehr interessant. Manchmal aber auch ein wenig stressig.
5 ____________________________?
– Ja, ich habe Kinder. Eine Tochter und zwei Söhne.
6 ____________________________?
– Ja, ich bin seit fast 10 Jahren verheiratet.
7 ____________________________?
– Ich sehe gern Filme und ich schwimme auch viel.
8 ____________________________?
– Nein, ich spreche kein Spanisch. Ich spreche aber sehr gut Englisch.

Exercise 7.4

Translate the following questions. Use both the **du** and **Sie** forms for 'you'.

1 What is your name?
2 Where do you come from?
3 What is your email address?
4 What is the time?
5 Are you married?
6 Do you have children?
7 Do you speak English?
8 What does he do for a living?

Checklist

1 Which question word do you use when you ask for a name or an address?
2 Where do you put the verb in a *yes or no question*?
3 Where do you put the verb in a *wh-question*?
4 If motion to or from a place is indicated, which two question words do you need to use?

UNIT 8
Articles

Two types of articles

Articles are normally used with nouns. There are two main types of articles in English and German: the *definite article*, which refers to someone or something that is specific or defined ('the woman', 'the house'), and the *indefinite article*, which refers to a noun that is not ('a woman', 'a house').

Articles signal the gender in German

English has the following articles: 'the' for the definite article, for both the singular and plural, and 'a'/'an' for the indefinite article.

As German has three genders (masculine, feminine and neuter), there are also different articles assigned to each gender:

	definite article	*indefinite article*
masculine	***der* Mann**	***ein* Mann**
feminine	***die* Frau**	***eine* Frau**
neuter	***das* Kind**	***ein* Kind**
plural	***die* Kinder**	**– Kinder**

Note that all three groups take the same definite article in the plural. Here are the two types in more detail.

The definite article

Referring to a specific noun

Like in English, the definite article is used in German with a noun when referring to a specific person, thing or concept:

***Der* Mann heißt Nicolai.**	The man is called Nicolai.
***Der* Kaffee schmeckt gut.**	The coffee tastes good.

***Die* Frau kommt aus Leipzig.**	The women comes from Leipzig.
***Die* Idee ist gut.**	The idea is good.
***Das* Kind ist fünf Jahre alt.**	The child is five years old.
***Die* Kinder sind 12 und 14.**	The children are 12 and 14.
***Die* Autos sind neu.**	The cars are new.

Articles are linked to gender

While in English you can simply use 'the' for all nouns, in German you'll need to use the article that is associated with the gender of the noun:

der – for masculine nouns
die – for feminine nouns
das – for neuter nouns

In the plural, the three forms have the same article: **die Jungen** 'the boys', **die Frauen** 'the women', **die Ideen** 'the ideas', **die Kinder** 'the children'.

Different usage

Although there are lots of similarities in the way the definite article is used in English and German, there are also some differences. In German, you'll need the definite articles:

- with masculine and feminine countries, such as **der Irak** 'Iraq', **der Iran** 'Iran', **die Schweiz** 'Switzerland', **die Türkei** 'Turkey':

  ***Die* Schweiz hat viele Berge.** — Switzerland has lots of mountains.

- for months and seasons, such as **der Sommer** 'the summer', **der Frühling** 'spring', **der Januar** 'January', **der Juni** 'June':

  ***Der* Sommer war schön.** — Summer was nice.
  ***Der* Januar war kalt.** — January was cold.

- for street names and names of parks:

  Ist das *die* Goethestraße? — Is this Goethestraße?
  ***Der* Central Park ist groß.** — Central Park is big.

- in expressions relating to institutions, such as schools and universities:

  Julian geht in *die* Grundschule. — Julian goes to primary school.
  Ich gehe heute in *die* Universität. — I am going to university today.

- with abstract nouns such as **das Leben** 'life', **die Natur** 'nature' or **die Kultur** 'culture':

  ***Das* Leben ist schön.** — Life is beautiful.
  Er liebt *die* Natur. — He loves nature.

However, when saying that someone plays an instrument, you don't use the definite article in German: **Björn spielt Klavier und Gitarre.** 'Björn plays the piano and the guitar.'

The indefinite article

Referring to an unspecific noun

The indefinite article refers to an unspecific person, thing or concept:

***Ein* Mann trinkt Kaffee.**	A man is drinking coffee.
Hier ist *ein* Laptop.	Here is a laptop.
***Eine* Frau aus Leipzig wohnt hier.**	A woman from Leipzig lives here.
Das ist *eine* gute Idee.	That's a good idea.
***Ein* Kind braucht viel Zuwendung.**	A child needs a lot of attention.
Das ist *ein* neues Computerspiel.	This is a new computer game.

Articles signal gender

As with the definite article, the indefinite article signals or in some ways 'determines' the gender of the noun that it is connected to:

ein – for masculine nouns
eine – for female nouns
ein – for neuter nouns

Note that there are no plural forms of the indefinite article.

Usage in German and English

Indefinite articles are used in a very similar way in the two languages, but there are several circumstances where German usage differs from that in English, including

- reference to nationality or affiliation with a city:

Er ist Amerikaner.	He's an American.
Ich bin Berliner.	I'm a Berliner.

- reference to occupation and religion:

Leon ist Rechtsanwalt.	Leon is a lawyer.
Carole ist Katholikin.	Carole is a Catholic.
Er ist Muslim.	He is a Muslim.

However, when appearing with an adjective, the indefinite article needs to be used:

Er ist *ein* typischer Amerikaner.	He's a typical American.
Leon ist *ein* guter Rechtsanwalt.	Leon is a good lawyer.

Das as a demonstrative

Das can also function as a demonstrative, i.e. pointing out single items, in the sense of 'this is …', 'that is …', 'these/those are …'.

***Das* ist der Manager.**	This/That is the manager.
***Das* ist die neue Apple Watch.**	This/That is the new Apple Watch.
***Das* sind die Spieler.**	These/Those are the players.

As you can see **das** doesn't change in this structure and has the same form in the singular and plural.

An alternative to **das** in this context is **dies**:

***Dies* ist der Manager.**	This/That is the manager.
***Dies* ist das Brandenburger Tor.**	This/That is the Brandenburg Gate.
***Dies* sind meine Notizen.**	These/Those are my notes.

Articles and cases

So far in this unit, articles have been linked to nouns that were almost entirely *the subject* of the sentence. However, nouns can also be the *direct* or *indirect object*. If this happens, the endings of the definite and indefinite articles change to reflect the specific role und function of the noun within a sentence.

All these changes are associated with the *case system* in German. The four cases and their effect on the articles are explained in detail in Units 11–15.

Did you know?

The definite and indefinite articles belong to a group of words which are called *determiners*. Other determiners are possessive adjectives, such as **mein** 'my', **dein** 'your', **sein** 'his', and **unser** 'our', and the negative **kein** 'no'. Determiners accompany nouns and follow a common pattern when used in more complex grammatical structures.

- For more information on articles and cases see Units 11–15.
- For gender of nouns see Unit 9.

Exercise 8.1

Supply the missing definite article: **der**, **die**, **das** or the plural **die**.

Example: Wie heißt ___ Sohn? → Wie heißt ***der*** Sohn?

1 ___ Frau kommt aus Brasilien.
2 ___ Idee ist wirklich gut.

3 Wie heißt ___ Junge?
4 ___ Mann von Elena ist aus München.
5 ___ Handy ist teuer.
6 Da ist ___ Manager.
7 Ist dies ___ Kind von Tim?
8 ___ Sommer ist jetzt zu Ende.
9 ___ Türkei ist schön.
10 Was machen ___ Kinder?

Exercise 8.2

Complete the table with the missing articles.

	definite article	*indefinite article*
masculine	***der***	___
feminine	___	***eine***
neuter	___	___
plural	___	___

Exercise 8.3

Decide whether the definite or indefinite article is more appropriate in these sentences. Both forms are given in brackets.

Example: ___ Firma hat ein neues Logo. (die / eine)
→ ***Die*** Firma hat ein neues Logo.

1 ___ Kaffee ist stark. (der / ein)
2 Das ist ___ neues Computerspiel. (das / ein)
3 Canberra ist ___ Hauptstadt von Australien. (die / eine)
4 Ich möchte ___ Bier und ___ Cola, bitte. (das / ein; die / eine)
5 Hannover ist ___ Stadt in Deutschland. (die / eine)
6 ___ Restaurant ist sehr gut. (das / ein)

Exercise 8.4

Translate the following sentences.

1 The woman comes from Berlin.
2 The coffee tastes good.
3 The child is seven years old.
4 The children are playing football.

5 He's an American.
6 He is a teacher.
7 This is the Brandenburg Gate.
8 Spring was cold.

Checklist

1 Can you explain what the difference between the definite and indefinite article is?
2 Do you know the various German words for 'the' covered in this unit?
3 Can you name the indefinite articles introduced in this unit?
4 Do you know three instances where you would use a definite article in German but not in English?
5 How can you say 'This/That is …' and 'These/Those are …' in German?

UNIT 9
Nouns and gender

What is a noun?

A noun is a word used to name a person, an item or a concept: a woman, a car, democracy. In many languages, nouns have different genders – they can be masculine, feminine or neuter.

'Biological' gender in English

In English, the gender of nouns conforms to their status: things and concepts are neuter ('it'), female persons are feminine ('she'), and male persons are masculine ('he'). This can be seen as classifying nouns according to 'biological' gender. German, on the other hand, uses grammatical gender, which means that most nouns don't have any obvious gender assigned to them.

Three genders in German

In German, all nouns are masculine, feminine or neuter. They can be identified by the definite article ('the' in English), which is different for each gender: **der** is for masculine nouns, **die** for female nouns and **das** for neuter nouns:

Masculine		
der	***der* Mann**, ***der* Tisch**	the man, the table
Feminine		
die	***die* Frau**, ***die* Tür**	the woman, the door
Neuter		
das	***das* Kind**, ***das* Regal**	the child, the shelf

In the plural all three groups take the same article: **die Männer** 'the men', **die Frauen** 'the women', **die Kinder** 'the children'.

As you can see, it is easy to predict the gender for nouns where the natural gender is fairly clear: ***der*** **Mann** is masculine and ***die*** **Frau** feminine.

Unfortunately, for the majority of nouns the gender seems more difficult to work out. For instance the German words for 'table', 'door' and 'shelf' – all describing items of furniture – are masculine, feminine and neuter respectively. It is therefore advisable to learn a new noun together with its gender: ***der*** **Tisch**, ***die*** **Tür**, ***das*** **Regal**.

How to find the gender of a noun

In a good conventional dictionary the gender of a noun is usually indicated after the word. The most common abbreviations are *m* (masculine), *f* (feminine), *nt* (neuter). In online dictionaries the noun is usually preceded by the relevant article: **der**, **die** or **das**.

There are also some clues that can help you work out whether a noun is masculine, feminine or neuter. One is the ending of a noun. Additionally, there are certain groups whose nouns share the same gender. Here is an overview.

Clues for masculine nouns

Typical endings

The following endings usually indicate that a noun is masculine:

-ig	**der Hon*ig*, der Käf*ig***	honey, cage
-ismus	**der Ideal*ismus*, der Kapital*ismus***	idealism, capitalism
-ling	**der Früh*ling*, der Schmetter*ling***	spring, butterfly
-or	**der Mot*or*, der Katalysat*or***	engine, catalyst

Groups of nouns

There are also certain groups of nouns which are masculine. They include:

male persons	**der Vater, der Sohn**	father, son
names of days and months	**der Montag, der Juni**	Monday, June
names of seasons	**der Sommer, der Winter**	summer, winter
makes of cars	**der VW, der Jaguar**	VW, Jaguar
alcoholic drinks	**der Whisky, der Wein**	whisky, wine

'Beer' is an exception and neuter: **das Bier**.

Clues for feminine nouns

Typical feminine endings

The following endings usually indicate that a noun is feminine:

-ei	**die Bäcker*ei*, die Poliz*ei***	bakery, police
-enz	**die Intellig*enz*, die Differ*enz***	intelligence, difference
-heit	**die Frei*heit*, die Dumm*heit***	freedom, stupidity
-ie	**die Demokrat*ie*, die Fantas*ie***	democracy, imagination
-ik	**die Mus*ik*, die Fabr*ik***	music, factory
-ion	**die Nat*ion*, die Stat*ion***	nation, station
-keit	**die Schwierig*keit*, die Möglich*keit***	difficulty, possibility/ opportunity
-tät	**die Universi*tät*, die Reali*tät***	university, reality
-schaft	**die Mann*schaft*, die Land*schaft***	team, landscape
-ung	**die Wohn*ung*, die Zeit*ung***	flat, newspaper
-ur	**die Kult*ur*, die Tastat*ur***	culture, keyboard

Note also that about ninety per cent of nouns ending in **-e** are also feminine: **die Adresse** 'address', **die Frage** 'question', **die Karriere** 'career'.

But there are a number of important exceptions such as **der Name** 'name' and **der Käse** 'cheese'.

Groups of nouns

Nouns which tend to be feminine are those for:

female persons	**die Mutter, die Tochter**	mother, daughter
names of motorbikes and ships	**die BMW, die Titanic**	BMW, *Titanic*
names of trees and flowers	**die Eiche, die Rose**	oak tree, rose

An important exception is **das Mädchen** 'girl'.

Clues for neuter nouns

Typical endings

As before with the other two genders, certain endings help you identify that a noun is neuter. The most important are:

-al	**das Materi*al*, das Potenzi*al***	material, potential
-chen	**das Mäd*chen*, das Mär*chen***	girl, fairy tale
-lein	**das Fräu*lein*, das Männ*lein***	miss, little man
-ma	**das Kli*ma*, das The*ma***	climate, theme/topic
-ment	**das Doku*ment*, das Instru*ment***	document, instrument
-o	**das Bür*o*, das Kont*o***	office, account
-um	**das Alb*um*, das Zentr*um***	album, centre

Important exceptions include: die Firma 'company'.

Groups of nouns

There are also certain groups of nouns which tend to be neuter:

young persons	**das Baby, das Kind**	baby, child
names of hotels and cinemas	**das Hilton, das Roxy**	the Hilton, the Roxy
names of most metals	**das Silber, das Gold**	silver, gold
infinitives used as nouns	**das Singen, das Tanzen**	singing, dancing

Compound nouns

You may have noticed that German speakers often use long words. In grammar terms a word that is made up of more than one noun is called a compound noun. In this case the last noun defines the gender:

die Reise + ***der Pass***	→	***der* Reise*pass***	passport
das Hand + ***die Nummer***		***die* Handy*nummer***	mobile number
der Computer + ***das Spiel***		***das* Computer*spiel***	computer game

Nouns take capital letters in German

Remember that all nouns in German start with a capital letter:

Das *N*otebook hat eine neue *T*astatur.	The notebook has a new keyboard.
Wie heißt das *K*ino?	What is the name of the cinema?
Die *S*tadt hat 3,6 *M*illionen *E*inwohner.	The city has 3.6 million inhabitants.

The initial capital letter can help you spot nouns in sentences and texts.

Summary of gender identifiers

Here is a summary of the main clues that can help you identify the gender of a noun in German:

masculine nouns **(der)**	*feminine nouns* **(die)**	*neuter nouns* **(das)**
Male persons Names of days and months Names of seasons Makes of cars Alcoholic drinks	Female persons Names of motorbikes and ships Names of trees and flowers	Young persons Names of hotels and cinemas Names of most metals Infinitives used as nouns
endings are:		
-ig, **-ismus**, **-ling**, **-or**	**-ei**, **-enz**, **-heit**, **-ie**, **-ik**, **-ion**, **-keit**, **-tät**, **-schaft**, **-ung**, **-ur**	**-al**, **-chen**, **-lein**, **-ma**, **-ment**, **-o**, **-um**

Did you know?

Many masculine nouns referring to people and professions have a feminine equivalent. Usually this is formed by adding **-in** to the male form:

der Freund	→	**die Freund*in***	**der Designer**	→	**die Designer*in***
der Student		**die Student*in***	**der Sozialarbeiter**		**die Sozialarbeiter*in***

It is important to use the correct form when referring to male and female descriptors and job titles. It would be quite inappropriate to use male forms for both men and women.

- For more details on articles and on how they can change in more complex structures see Unit 8 and Units 11–15.

Exercise 9.1

Here are groups of nouns. Do you remember which article they take?

Example: ____ Hilton, Ritz, Vierjahreszeiten-Hotel
→ ***das*** Hilton, Ritz, Vierjahreszeiten-Hotel

1 ____ Montag, Dienstag, Mittwoch, Sonntag
2 ____ Audi, Ferrari, Nissan, Ford
3 ____ Silber, Gold, Eisen, Kupfer
4 ____ Rose, Tulpe, Sonnenblume

5 ____ Tochter, Schwester, Mutter, Cousine
6 ____ Sommer, Frühling, Herbst, Winter
7 ____ Wodka, Champagner, Rotwein, Schnaps
8 ____ Schwimmen, Essen, Tanzen, Joggen

Exercise 9.2

Decide whether the nouns in the box are masculine, feminine or neuter and put either *m*, *f* or *nt* in the appropriate box. Most words have appeared previously, but if you are not sure about the meaning, check in an online or conventional dictionary. The first two have been done.

Bäckerei	*f*	Auto		Flasche		Temperatur	
Lampe	*f*	Märchen		Metzgerei		Museum	
Kirche		Emigration		Zentrum		Religion	
Liberalismus		Nation		Demokratie		Instrument	
Zeitung		Kino		Büro		Potenzial	
Meinung		Honig		Universität		Motor	
Karte		Optimismus		Mädchen		Natur	

Now make a list of the typical (1) *masculine*, (2) *feminine* and (3) *neuter* endings that have appeared in the examples above.

masculine	*feminine*	*neuter*

Exercise 9.3

Rewrite the following sentences and put a capital letter where necessary. Remember that all German sentences start with a capital letter.

Example: berlin hat eine lange geschichte.
→ ***B***erlin hat eine lange ***G***eschichte.

1 berlin ist eine fantastische stadt.
2 das hotel liegt sehr zentral.
3 der service ist ausgezeichnet und das essen ist gut.
4 die woche geht so schnell vorbei.

5 die menschen in berlin sind sehr freundlich.
6 heute abend gehen wir zuerst in ein konzert und dann in ein restaurant und feiern unseren letzten tag in berlin.

Exercise 9.4

Are the nouns masculine, feminine or neuter? Fill in the missing definite article (der, die or das).

Example: ____ Essen schmeckt sehr gut. → ***Das*** Essen schmeckt sehr gut.

1 ____ E-Auto fährt sehr ökologisch.
2 ____ Tisch und ____ Regal sind kaputt.
3 ____ Tochter heißt Marina.
4 ____ Rose ist sehr schön.
5 ____ Karte kostet 10 Euro.
6 ____ Jacke ist von Chanel.
7 ____ Bier ist alkoholfrei.
8 ____ Stadtzentrum ist sehr alt.
9 Ist ____ VW neu?
10 ____ Mädchen ist elf Jahre alt und ____ Junge ist sieben.
11 ____ Internetverbindung ist sehr langsam.
12 ____ Grammatik ist manchmal schwer.

Checklist

1 Can you name at least two typical endings for masculine nouns, five endings for feminine nouns and two for neuter nouns?
2 Do you know some groups of nouns or categories where nouns share the same gender?
3 In a compound noun that consists of more than one noun, which one defines the gender of the whole word?
4 What is distinctive about the spelling of German nouns?

UNIT 10
Plural of nouns

Singular and plural

When nouns refer to only one item they are grammatically in the singular form. If you talk about more than one item you use the plural: **ein Auto** 'a car' (singular) → **zwei Autos** 'two cars' (plural).

Plurals in English

In English it is relatively easy to form the plural forms of nouns – normally you only add '-s':

'a house' → 'five house*s*', 'an idea' → 'two ideas'

Exceptions include 'a woman' → 'two women', 'a child' → 'three children'.

Patterns in German

German has several ways of forming the plural. It is therefore advisable to learn a new word with its plural form. But as with gender, there are patterns for typical endings or plural formations for masculine, feminine and neuter nouns. Here is an overview.

Clues for masculine nouns

Adding **-e**

The majority of masculine nouns form their plural by just adding **-e**:

singular		*plural*		*ending: -e*
der Tisch	table	**die Tisch*e***	tables	**-e**
der Beruf	job	**die Beruf*e***	jobs	**-e**
der Tag	day	**die Tag*e***	days	**-e**

Adding an umlaut + -e

Often an umlaut + **-e** is added when the original stem vowel is **a** or **u**:

singular		*plural*		*ending: umlaut + -e*
der Zug	train	**die Z*ü*g*e***	trains	umlaut + **-e**
der Supermarkt	supermarket	**die Superm*ä*rkt*e***	supermarkets	umlaut + **-e**

Always remember that these are only guidelines; there are some irregular endings such as **der Mann → die Männer**.

Clues for feminine nouns

Adding -n or -en

The huge majority of feminine nouns add **-n** or **-en**:

singular		*plural*		*ending: -n or -en*
die Tasse	cup	**die Tasse*n***	cups	**-n**
die Sprache	language	**die Sprache*n***	languages	**-n**
die Frau	woman	**die Frau*en***	women	**-en**
die Zeitung	newspaper	**die Zeitung*en***	newspapers	**-en**

Adding umlaut + -e

A number of commonly used feminine nouns add an umlaut + **-e**:

singular		*plural*		*ending: umlaut + -e*
die Hand	hand	**die H*ä*nd*e***	hands	umlaut + **-e**
die Stadt	city	**die St*ä*dt*e***	cities	umlaut + **-e**

Again be aware that there are different forms. **Mutter** and **Tochter**, for instance, both only add an umlaut: **die Mutter → die Mütter**, **die Tochter → die Töchter**.

Clues for neuter nouns

Adding -e

Most neuter nouns add **-e** but no umlaut:

singular		*plural*		*ending: -e*
das Haar	hair	**die Haar*e***	hairs	**-e**
das Jahr	year	**die Jahr*e***	years	**-e**

singular		*plural*		*ending: -e*
das Angebot	offer	**die Angebot*e***	offers	**-e**
das Programme	programme	**die Programm*e***	programmes	**-e**

Adding umlaut + ***-er***

Another common ending is **-er**, with an umlaut where the original stem vowel is **a**, **o** or **u**:

singular		*plural*		*ending: -er or umlaut + -er*
das Kind	child	**die Kind*er***	children	**-er**
das Land	country	**die L*ä*nd*er***	countries	umlaut + **-er**
das Buch	book	**die B*ü*ch*er***	books	umlaut + **-er**

Nouns ending in ***-chen*** *or* ***-lein***

Nouns ending in **-chen** or **-lein** do not change in the plural:

singular		*plural*		*no ending*
das Mädchen	girl	**die Mädchen**	girls	–

Nouns ending in *-er*, *-el* or *-en*

Nouns ending in **-er**, **-el** or **-en**, regardless whether they are masculine, feminine or neuter, do not change but sometimes add an umlaut:

singular		*plural*		*no ending or just umlaut*
der Kuchen	cake	**die Kuchen**	cakes	–
das Zimmer	room	**die Zimmer**	rooms	–
der Apfel	apple	**die *Ä*pfel**	apples	umlaut
die Tochter	daughter	**die T*ö*chter**	daughters	umlaut

An exception is **Schwester** 'sister' which adds **-n**: **die Schwester → die Schwester*n***.

Foreign words

Foreign word which are 'imported' into German from English or French usually add **-s**:

der Blog	blog	**die Blog*s***	blogs
das Büro	office	**die Büro*s***	offices
das E-Book	e-book	**die E-Book*s***	e-books
der Park	park	**die Park*s***	parks

How to find the plural from a dictionary

If you do not know the plural form of a noun you can look it up in a conventional dictionary. The plural form is usually given in third place, after the *gender* and the *genitive ending* – each of these separated by a comma:

Beruf *m*, **-(e)s**, **-e** profession, occupation	→	Here the plural is given as **-e**: **Beruf*e*.**
Reise *f*, **-**, **-n** journey, trip	→	Here the plural is given as **-n**: **Reise*n*.**

If you look up the plural of a noun and see ¨-, this means that an umlaut is needed:

Vater *m*, **-s**, **¨-** father	→	The plural should therefore be **V*ä*ter.**

In some cases an umlaut plus ending is required:

Hand *f*, **-**, **¨-e** hand	→	Here you have to add an umlaut plus **-e**: **Hand** becomes **H*ä*nd*e*.**

In online dictionaries, the plural form is often given in full.

Points to remember

Here is a summary of the most common plural noun endings:

-e	Most masculine nouns need an extra **-e**: **der Tag → die Tag*e***
	The same applies to neuter nouns: **das Bier → die Bier*e***
-e + *umlaut*	Many masculine nouns also add an umlaut: **der Supermarkt → die Superm*ä*rkt*e***
	So do a number of feminine nouns: **die Hand → die H*ä*nd*e***
-er *(+ umlaut)*	Many neuter nouns add umlaut + **-er** when possible: **das Buch → die B*ü*ch*er***
	A few masculine nouns also have the same changes: **der Wald → die W*ä*ld*er***

-e	Most masculine nouns need an extra **-e**: **der Tag → die Tag*e***
-n *or* ***-en***	Around ninety per cent of feminine nouns follow this pattern:
	die Sprache → die Sprache*n*
	die Frau → die Fraue*n*
-s	Most foreign words in German take **-s**: **die Party → die Party*s***
No ending	Nouns ending with **-chen** or **-lein**: **das Mädchen → die Mädchen**
	Nouns ending with **-el**, **-en**, **-er**: **der Spiegel → die Spiegel**
	Often they just add an umlaut: **der Vater → die V*ä*ter**

Did you know?

When forming the plural of nouns imported from English which end in **-y**, in German you simply add an **-s**; the forms don't end in '-ies' as in English:

Was für Hobbys haben Sie?	What sort of hobbies do you have?
Er hat zwei Hardcopys gemacht.	He made two hard copies.
Sie geht auf zwei Partys.	She is going to two parties.

Exercise 10.1

Use the given information and write out the plural form of the following nouns. The first one has been done.

1	Messer *nt*, -	***die Messer***
2	Mantel *m*, ¨	die Mäntel
3	Buch *nt*, ¨er	die Bücher
4	Kühlschrank *m*, ¨e	die Kühlschränke
5	Glas *nt*, ¨er	die Gläser
6	Mutter *f*, ¨	____
7	Passwort *nt*, ¨er	____
8	Regal *nt*, -e	____
9	Tasse *f*, -n	____
10	Teppich *m*, -e	____
11	Zeitung *f*, -en	____
12	Zimmer *nt*, -	____

Exercise 10.2

Give the plural form of the following nouns.

Example: die Flasche → die Flaschen

1 der Tag → die ____
2 der Kurs die ____
3 der Orangensaft die ____
4 der Gast die ____
5 der Schnaps die ____
6 die Tasse die ____
7 die Tomate die ____
8 die Meinung die ____
9 die Stadt die ____
10 die Bratwurst die ____
11 das Schiff die ____
12 das Programm die ____
13 das Haus die ____
14 das Buch die ____
15 das Land die ____
16 das Hotel die ____
17 der Blog die ____
18 das Handy die Handys
19 der Tweet die Tweets
20 der Sneaker die Sneakers

Exercise 10.3

Now go through the plural forms again and identify the typical (1) *masculine*, (2) *neuter* and (3) *feminine* endings used in Exercise 10.2.

masculine	*feminine*	*neuter*

Exercise 10.4

Translate the following sentences.

1 I would like two bottles, please.
2 Two sausages, please.
3 The apples are very sweet.
4 He has two sisters and three brothers.
5 She reads three newspapers.
6 The house has four rooms.
7 The houses are new.
8 She speaks five languages.
9 He has three mobile phones.
10 The parties are always interesting.

Checklist

1 What are the two most common plural endings for masculine nouns?
2 How do almost all feminine nouns form their plural?
3 What are the most common plural endings for neuter nouns?
4 How do most foreign (imported) words form the plural? Just add an S.
5 Where do you find information on how the plural is formed in a conventional dictionary? It will tell u if there's an umlaut + if you have to add any letters eg -e, -en, -er etc. This comes after the Genitive ending.

UNIT 11
The four cases

This unit will give you a short overview of the basic rules governing the cases in German and compare them to their usage in English. Units 12–15 will explain each case in detail and give examples and exercises.

What are cases?

Nouns (words such as 'man', 'house' and 'dog') play different roles in a sentence or clause. For example a noun can be the agent of what is happening ('The *dog* bites the man'), or it can be in the position where the action of the verb happens to it ('The dog bites the *man*'). In German, these different roles are signalled by the *case*. The different cases are shown in the endings of words which accompany the nouns, such as the articles 'the' and 'a'.

How does this compare to English?

In English, the noun also plays these different roles in the sentence. You know that a noun is a subject when it comes *before* the verb. If it is an object, it comes *after* the verb. But normally, the case therein isn't evident, except when you use pronouns like 'he' or 'she':

Peter loves Mary.	He loves *her*.
Mary loves Peter.	She loves *him*.

The four cases in German

There are four different cases in German. Each case can be linked to a particular role, or 'function', in the sentence.

The nominative case

The nominative is used when the noun is the subject of the sentence, i.e. the 'agent' of what is happening ('Who or what is doing the action?'):

Der Mann liest. *The man* is reading.

The accusative case

When the noun is the direct object, i.e. the 'receiver' or 'target' of the action in the sentence, German normally uses the accusative ('Who or what is affected by the action?'):

Der Mann liest _den Roman._ The man is reading *the novel.*

The dative case

In addition to the direct object, many verbs can take a second object, the indirect object ('To whom/what, or for whom/what is the action done?').

Der Mann gibt _dem Freund_ einen Roman.
The man gives *the friend* a novel. / The man gives the novel *to a friend.*

The genitive case

This is used to show the relationship between two nouns. It indicates that one item 'belongs' to the other.

Der Hut _des Mannes..._ *The man's* hat...

Why are cases important?

The four cases in German dictate the endings of definite articles ('the' – **der**, **die**, **das**), indefinite articles ('a' – **ein**, **eine**, **ein**) and other words linked with nouns (see Units 12–15 for more).

Can you spot the changes for the masculine definite article when linked to different cases in the examples above?

Answer: **d*er* Mann** = nominative; **d*en* Roman** = accusative; **d*em* Freund** = dative; **d*es* Mannes** = genitive.

Similarly, the definite feminine and neuter and plural articles change when used in different case structures (see below).

Overview of article changes

Here is an overview of how the four cases affect the definite and the indefinite articles.

The definite article

	nominative	*accusative*	*dative*	*genitive*
masculine	**der**	**d*en***	**d*em***	**d*es***
feminine	**die**	**die**	**d*er***	**d*er***
neuter	**das**	**das**	**d*em***	**d*es***
plural	**die**	**die**	**d*en***	**d*er***

The indefinite article

	nominative	*accusative*	*dative*	*genitive*
masculine	**ein**	**ein*en***	**ein*em***	**ein*es***
feminine	**eine**	**eine**	**ein*er***	**ein*er***
neuter	**ein**	**ein**	**ein*em***	**ein*es***

If you look more closely you will see that, apart from the masculine form, the nominative and accusative are identical. There are also patterns for the dative and genitive which will be explained in the following units.

Factors which determine cases

There are three factors which determine case. We have explained one of them above: the case is determined by the role the noun plays in the sentence; is it a subject or an object?

There are two more factors which decide which case must be used: the verb and prepositions in the sentence.

Verbs

The verb determines which case you use for the object:

- The majority of verbs require the accusative.
- Certain verbs always require the dative (for example **helfen** 'to help' or **gehören** 'to belong').
- Very few verbs take the genitive case.

If you have a verb which requires the dative case, then the object in the German sentence needs to be in the dative:

Der Mann hilft *der* Frau.	The man helps the woman.

In this German sentence, 'the woman' is in the dative case (***der* Frau**) because with the verb ***helfen*** the object is in the dative.

Prepositions

Prepositions (words such as 'at', 'on', 'to' and 'for') require a certain case in German.

- Some of them are followed by the accusative, for example **durch** 'through' or **für** 'for'.
- Some prepositions require the dative, for example **mit** 'with' or **von** 'from'.
- Very few prepositions take the genitive.

If you have a preposition which requires the accusative case, then the following object in the German sentence *must* be in the accusative:

Ich kaufe ein Geschenk für meinen Freund.	I'm buying a present for my friend.

In English, 'for my friend' is the indirect object, but in German **meinen Freund** is in the accusative case because **für** is one of the prepositions after which you must always use the accusative.

Summary of basic principles

The use of cases is determined by three principles:

- the role of the noun – whether it is the subject or object of the sentence
- the verb
- any prepositions used.

It is particularly important to learn which verbs take the dative, and which prepositions are followed by which case.

Did you know?

Cases are an important feature in many languages. In addition to the nominative, accusative, dative and genitive, which are also used in German, Latin had two other main cases: the vocative, used when addressing people, and the ablative, relating to motion.

Some living languages such as Russian and Hungarian contain even more cases, with Finnish at the top end, having 15 of them.

Exercise 11.1

Underline the subject – the noun in the *nominative* – in each sentence.

Example: Die Frau isst einen Hamburger.
→ <u>Die Frau</u> isst einen Hamburger.

1 Der Mann geht ins Fitnesscenter.
2 Das Kind spielt mit dem I-Pad.
3 In der Garage steht das Auto.
4 Die Tochter sieht einen Clip auf YouTube.
5 Um acht Uhr verlässt die Nachbarin das Haus.
6 Nach dem Essen trinken die Leute noch Kaffee.

Exercise 11.2

Identify the objects in the following sentences and number them 1 and 2. Can you identify which object is in the accusative and which one in the dative case?

Example: Sie gibt dem Mann eine Karte. → dem Mann (1), eine Karte (2)

(1) **dem Mann** is in the dative case (something is given to him)
(2) **eine Karte** is in the accusative case

1 Ich schenke der Frau ein Buch.
2 Er kauft dem Mädchen ein Eis.
3 Herr Schulz zeigt dem Gast den Garten.
4 Der Kellner bringt dem Mann das Essen.

Exercise 11.3

In the two tables below, put a tick next to those articles which have different endings to the nominative forms. One of each has been done.

The indefinite article

	accusative		*dative*		*genitive*	
masculine	**einen**		**einem**		**eines**	
feminine	**eine**		**einer**		**einer**	
neuter	**ein**		**einem**	✓	**eines**	

The definite article

	accusative		*dative*		*genitive*	
masculine	**den**	✓	**dem**		**des**	
feminine	**die**		**der**		**der**	
neuter	**das**		**dem**		**des**	

Checklist

1 Can you list the three principles that determine the cases in German?
2 Which case do you use for the subject?
3 Which case do you use for the direct object?
4 Which case do you use for the indirect object?
5 Which words linked to nouns are affected by the different cases?

UNIT 12
The nominative case

What is the nominative case?

German uses the nominative case if the noun is the subject in a sentence – a person or thing doing the action.

Examples:

Here are some examples of nouns in the nominative case:

Der Mann **hört Musik.**	*The man* is listening to music.
Die Frau **liest das Magazin.**	*The woman* reads the magazine.
Das Kind **kauft einen Keks.**	*The child* buys a cookie.
Die Gäste **wollen es nicht.**	*The guests* don't want it.

Endings in the nominative case

As described in Unit 11, cases are important in German because they affect the endings of various words linked to nouns. Apart from articles, these include possessives ('my', 'your' etc.) and the negative **kein** 'no'. In grammatical terms, this group of words is referred to as *determiners*. Here is an overview of determiners in the nominative:

	masculine	*feminine*	*neuter*	*plural*
definite articles	***der*** **Mann**	***die*** **Frau**	***das*** **Kind**	***die*** **Gäste**
indefinite articles	***ein*** **Mann**	***eine*** **Frau**	***ein*** **Kind**	**— Gäste**
possessive	***mein*** **Mann**	***meine*** **Frau**	***mein*** **Kind**	***meine*** **Gäste**
negative	***kein*** **Mann**	***keine*** **Frau**	***kein*** **Kind**	***keine*** **Gäste**

The nominative case after *sein* and *werden*

Note that you also use the nominative after **sein** 'to be' and **werden** 'to become':

Er ist *ein* interessanter Mann.	He is an interesting man.
Der Wagen ist *ein* BMW.	The car is a BMW.
Es wird *ein* schöner Tag.	It's going to be a nice day.

However, this is not always obvious, since you sometimes do not use an indefinite article with these verbs in German:

Er ist Ingenieur.	He is an engineer.
Sie wird Sportlehrerin.	She is going to be(come) a PE teacher.

How to spot the nominative case

The subject does not have to be at the beginning of the sentence:

Morgen fährt *die Klasse* nach Berlin.	Tomorrow the class is going to Berlin.
Zum Frühstück trinkt *er* grünen Tee.	For breakfast he drinks green tea.

An easy way to find out the subject of a sentence is to ask, 'Who or what is doing the action?' Who is going to Berlin tomorrow? The class. Who is drinking green tea? He is.

Did you know?

According to research carried out by *Duden*, seen by many as the authority in matters of German grammar and spelling, the nominative articles **der**, **die**, **das** are the three words which occur most frequently in German texts.

The top most commonly used words are (1) **der**, **die**, **das**; (2) **in**; (3) **und**; (4) **sein**; and (5) **ein**.

Exercise 12.1

Fill in the correct form of the indefinite (**ein**, **eine**, **ein**) and definite articles (**der**, **die**, **das**, plural **die**) in the nominative. The genders of the nouns are given in brackets.

Example: (*f*) Dies ist ***eine*** Popband. ***Die*** Popband heißt *Schiller*.

1 (*m*) Dies ist ____ LED-Fernseher. ____ LED-Fernseher kostet 400 Euro.
2 (*nt*) Dies ist ____ Auto. ____ Auto ist ein VW.

3 (*f*) Dies ist ____ Zeitung. ____ Zeitung heißt *Die Welt*.
4 (*f*) Dies ist ____ Flasche Bier. ____ Flasche kommt aus München.
5 (*nt*) Dies ist ____ Hotel. ____ Hotel heißt Maritim.
6 (*m*) Dies ist ____ Supermarkt. ____ Supermarkt heißt Aldi.
7 (*pl*) Dies sind Studenten. ____ Studenten kommen aus Kanada.
8 (*pl*) Dies sind Trainers. ____ Trainers sind neu.

Exercise 12.2

Underline the subject in the following sentences.

Example: Am Wochenende spielt sie meistens Fußball.
→ Am Wochenende spielt sie meistens Fußball.

1 Morgen fahren wir nach Italien.
2 Meine Mutter heißt Svenja.
3 Hast du heute Zeit?
4 Im Sommer wohnen wir in Berlin.
5 Trinkt er gern Wein?
6 Hier ist die Musik sehr laut.
7 Nächsten Monat gehe ich in ein Konzert.

Exercise 12.3

Translate the following sentences.

1 This is a house.
2 The house is very old.
3 The man is called Mario.
4 The newspaper is very interesting.
5 Edeka is a supermarket in Germany.
6 My wife works in Hamburg.
7 Where are the children?

Checklist

1 What function does the noun have in a sentence when it is in the nominative case?
2 After which two verbs do you use the nominative?
3 How can you spot the subject in a sentence?
4 Can you name the determiner endings in the nominative?

UNIT 13
The accusative case

What is the accusative case?

German normally uses the accusative case when the noun is the direct object in the sentence, i.e. the 'receiver' or 'target' of the action:

Der Mann kauft *den Computer*.	The man buys the computer.
Ich möchte *einen Kaffee*, bitte.	I'd like a coffee, please.

Masculine forms change

In the accusative case, the endings for the determiners change when used for masculine nouns. For feminine, neuter and plural nouns the accusative endings are the same as in the nominative case.

For masculine nouns:

- **der** changes to **den** and
- **ein** changes to **einen**

Endings in the accusative case

Here is an overview of accusative endings for the most common determiners:

determiners	*masculine*	*feminine*	*neuter*	*plural*
definite articles	***den* Mann**	***die* Frau**	***das* Kind**	***die* Gäste**
indefinite articles	***einen* Mann**	***eine* Frau**	***ein* Kind**	**— Gäste**
possessive	***meinen* Mann**	***meine* Frau**	***mein* Kind**	***meine* Gäste**
negative	***keinen* Mann**	***keine* Frau**	***kein* Kind**	***keine* Gäste**

As you can see, the endings for all masculine determiners are **-en**.

Examples:

Here are some examples of nouns in the accusative case in use:

nominative	*accusative*	
der Podcast (*m*)	**Ich höre *den* Podcast.**	I am listening to the podcast.
die Mütze (*f*)	**Er trägt *die* Mütze.**	He is wearing the cap.
das Auto (*nt*)	**Fährst du *das* Auto?**	Are you driving the car?
ein Regenschirm (*m*)	**Ich habe *einen* Regenschirm.**	I've got an umbrella.
eine Cola (*f*)	**Ich möchte *eine* Cola.**	I'd like a coke.
ein Mineralwasser (*nt*)	**Sie trinkt *ein* Mineralwasser.**	She is drinking a mineral water.
der Hunger (*m*)	**Ich habe *keinen* Hunger.**	I'm not hungry.
ihr Bruder (*m*)	**Sie vermisst *ihren* Bruder.**	She misses her brother.

The accusative case after most verbs

You use the accusative after most verbs in German. Verbs which take the accusative are also called *transitive verbs*. In a conventional dictionary, you often see the abbreviation '*vt*' after the headword, which indicates that this verb takes the accusative.

In online dictionaries this is normally not shown.

The accusative case after prepositions

You also use the accusative case after certain prepositions. The following prepositions always take the accusative:

bis	until
durch	through
für	for
gegen	around (for time)
ohne	without
um	around, at

Examples:

Wir fahren gerade durch *einen* Tunnel.	We are just driving through a tunnel.

Arbeitest du für *die* Firma?	Do you work for the company?
Er ist gegen *das* Angebot.	He is against the offer.
Sie kommt ohne *ihren* Freund.	She is coming without her boyfriend.

Remember that whenever you use one of the prepositions listed above, you *must* use the accusative form for the words linked to the following noun.

More than one accusative in a sentence

As explained above, the use of the accusative case is *not* only determined by the noun being in a position like the direct object in English. Use of the accusative case is also determined by the verb and some prepositions. It is therefore possible that there is more than one accusative form in a sentence:

Er trägt *den* Anzug ohne *eine* Krawatte.	He is wearing the suit without a tie.
Wir kaufen *einen* Tisch und *einen* Schrank für *deinen* Vater.	We are buying a table and a wardrobe for your father.

The accusative case – the main points

The accusative case is mainly used for the *direct object* in a sentence. But it can also be determined by the *verb* and *certain prepositions*.

Don't forget that, with feminine, neuter and plural nouns, the endings for the determiners do *not* change in the accusative and are exactly the same as in the nominative.

Did you know?

The accusative is also used in certain situations and expressions where its use doesn't seem obvious. For instance, when ordering food and drink, requests are often shortened and the first part of the sentence, i.e. **Ich möchte ...**, is omitted but implied:

Einen Kaffee, bitte.
Einen Tee und dann noch einen Butterkuchen, bitte.

- For more information on prepositions see Unit 25.
- For more information on pronouns in the accusative see Unit 16.
- For adjective endings in the accusative see Unit 26.

Exercise 13.1

You have moved house and still need a lot of things. Make sentences beginning with **Ich brauche** and use the correct endings in the accusative case.

Examples: der Computer → Ich brauche einen Computer.
die Tasche → Ich brauche eine Tasche.
das Kochbuch → Ich brauche ein Kochbuch.

1 die Lampe → ______________________
2 die Blumenvase → ______________________
3 der Küchentisch → ______________________
4 das Sofa → ______________________
5 das Bücherregal → ______________________
6 der Teppich → ______________________
7 der Kühlschrank → ______________________
8 die Mikrowelle → ______________________
9 die Kaffeemaschine → ______________________
11 die Waschmaschine → ______________________
10 das Handy → ______________________
12 der Camcorder → ______________________

What else do you need? For further practice make a list of things that you might also need. Check the new words and their gender in a dictionary.

Exercise 13.2

Fill in the correct endings after prepositions taking the accusative case. The gender is given in brackets.

Example: Er geht um d__ Haus. (*nt*) → Er geht um ***das*** Haus.

1 Das Buch ist für ein__ Freund. (*m*)
2 Das Sweatshirt ist für ein__ Freundin. (*f*)
3 Die Sportschuhe sind für mein__ Schwester. (*f*)
4 Die Socken sind für mein__ Vater. (*m*)
5 Die Lego-Spiele sind für d__ Kind. (*nt*)
6 Er ist gegen d__ Idee. (*f*)
7 Ohne d__ Hund möchte er nicht in den Urlaub fahren. (*m*)
8 Er möchte um d__ ganze Welt fahren. (*f*)

Exercise 13.3

Translate the following sentences.

1 I'd like a coffee.
2 The man buys the computer.
3 The woman buys the camcorder.

4 The child reads the book.
5 The sweatshirt is for my brother.
6 The book is for my sister.
7 We walk through the park.
8 I need a coffee machine and a microwave.
9 I need an umbrella.
10 I am for the idea.

Checklist

1 When do you use the accusative case?
2 In the accusative, which endings differ from the nominative forms?
3 When using a good conventional dictionary, how can you often find out whether a verb takes the accusative?
4 Can you name some prepositions which require the accusative case?

UNIT 14
The dative case

What is the dative case?

The dative case is mainly used for the indirect object, i.e. a person or thing for whom or to which something is done:

Sie schickt *dem Mann* eine SMS.	She sends *the man* a text message.
Der Lehrer gibt *der Frau* ein Buch.	The teacher gives *the woman* a book.
Yasmin kauft *dem Kind* ein Eis.	Yasmin buys *the child* an ice-cream.
Tim zeigt *den Gästen* die Umgebung.	Tim shows *the guests* the surroundings.

Changes in the dative case

In the dative case, the determiners, for example the definite and indefinite articles, are different to those of the nominative and accusative; however, they follow certain patterns. With the plural forms of nouns, you normally also need to add **-n**.

Endings in the dative case

Here is an overview of the dative forms for the most common determiners:

determiner	*masculine*	*feminine*	*neuter*	*plural*
definite article	**d*em* Mann**	**d*er* Frau**	**d*em* Kind**	**d*en* Gäste*n***
indefinite article	**ein*em* Mann**	**ein*er* Frau**	**ein*em* Kind**	**– Gäste*n***
possessive	**mein*em* Mann**	**mein*er* Frau**	**mein*em* Kind**	**mein*en* Gäste*n***
negative	**kein*em* Mann**	**kein*er* Frau**	**kein*em* Kind**	**kein*en* Gäste*n***

Note that

- the masculine and the neuter endings are the same: add **-em**
- for the feminine endings add -**er**.

Additional endings for plural nouns

For most plural forms in the dative, an additional **-n** is added to the noun:

die Gäste → den Gäste*n*
die Freunde → den Freunde*n*

When the plural ends in **-n** or **-s**, no addition is made: **die Menschen → den Menschen**; **die Laptops → den Laptops**.

Verbs which require the dative case

You use the dative after a few verbs. The most important ones are:

antworten 'to answer', **begegnen** 'to encounter, to meet', **helfen** 'to help', **danken** 'to thank', **gehören** 'to belong to', **gratulieren** 'to congratulate', **folgen** 'to follow', **trauen** 'to trust'.

Here are some of them in use:

der Mann	**Ich folge *dem* Mann.**	I follow the man.
die Mutter	**Er gratuliert *der* Mutter.**	He congratulates the mother.
das Kind	**Ich helfe *dem* Kind.**	I'm helping the child.
die Gäste	**Das I-Pad gehört *den* Gästen.**	The iPad belongs to the guests.

Try to learn these verbs by heart.

The dative after prepositions

The dative also follows after some prepositions. They are:

aus	from, out of
außer	apart from
bei	at, near

gegenüber	opposite
mit	with, by (for means of transport)
nach	after, to
seit	since, for
von	from
zu	to

Here are some of them in use:

Er kommt aus *der* Türkei.	He's from Turkey.
Er wohnt gegenüber *der* Kirche.	He lives opposite the church.
Ich fahre mit *dem* Bus.	I'll go by bus.
Nach *der* Arbeit gehe ich einkaufen.	After work, I'll go shopping.
Tim studiert seit *einem* Jahr.	Tim has been studying for one year.
Wir fahren zu *meiner* Freundin.	We'll go to my girlfriend's.

More than one dative in a sentence

Because the dative in German can be determined by the verb or by a preposition, it is not uncommon for it to appear more than once in a sentence or clause. Look at the following examples:

Sie gratulieren *dem* Fahrer zu *seinem* Sieg.
They congratulate the driver on his success.

Lara hilft *ihrer* Tochter mit *den* Hausaufgaben.
Lara helps her daughter with the homework.

The dative case – the main points

The dative case is mainly used for the *indirect object* in German. But it can also appear after certain *verbs* and after a number of *prepositions*.

All endings for the determiners differ from the nominative:

- masculine and neuter endings are **-em**.
- feminine endings are **-er**.
- plural endings are **-en** and often **-n** is added to the noun.

Did you know?

When stating where somebody or something is from, you normally use **aus** 'from'. If the place name has a gender in German or is in the plural, you'll need to use the appropriate dative form:

der Iran	→	**Er kommt aus *dem* Iran.**
die Türkei		**Der Wein kommt aus *der* Türkei.**
die USA (*pl.*)		**Das Tablet kommt aus *den* USA.**

- For more information on prepositions see Unit 25.
- For more information on pronouns in the dative see Unit 16.
- For adjective endings in the dative see Unit 26.

Exercise 14.1

Presents! Presents! Maria has been on an exchange visit. On her last day she gives her host family lots of presents. Write out what she gives to whom following the example.

Example: Großmutter → eine Schachtel Pralinen
→ Sie gibt ***der Großmutter*** eine Schachtel Pralinen.

1 Großvater → ein Buch über Nelson Mandela
2 Mutter → einen Strauß Blumen
3 Vater → eine Flasche Wein
4 Sohn → Star-Wars-Tasse
5 Tochter → ein Haarband
6 Baby → einen Ball

Exercise 14.2

Fill in the correct endings after prepositions and verbs taking the dative case.

Example: Fährst du zu dein__ Bruder?
→ Fährst du zu ***deinem*** Bruder?

1 Er fährt jeden Tag mit d__ Auto.
2 Gegenüber d__ Rathaus ist der Stadtpark.
3 Sie kommt gerade aus d__ Stadt.
4 Den neuen Shop gibt es seit ein__ Jahr.
5 Vor ein__ Woche hat sie geheiratet.
6 Was machst du heute nach d__ Arbeit?
7 Sie wohnt bei ein__ Freund.
8 Er telefoniert mit d__ Handy.
9 Sie hilft d__ Frau.
10 Das gehört d__ Mann.
11 Er dankt d__ 20 Mitarbeiter__.
12 Wir helfen d__ Kindern__.

Exercise 14.3

Translate the following sentences.

1 She gives the baby a book.
2 Paulina buys the child an ice-cream.
3 He gives the grandfather a bottle of wine.
4 He follows the man.
5 The iPad belongs to the driver.
6 Peter helps the girl.
7 He gives the children a football.
8 She comes from Turkey.

Checklist

1 Which three factors determine the use of the dative case?
2 Can you name the determiner endings for masculine and neuter nouns in the singular?
3 Do you know the endings for the feminine and plural determiners?
4 How are most plural nouns affected by the dative case?

UNIT 15

The genitive case

What is the genitive case?

The genitive case is used to indicate possession or ownership: **Das ist die Tasche *meines Vaters.*** 'That is *my father's* bag.'

What's different in German?

Usage in English and German is very similar. One main difference is the *word order*. Whereas in English the genitive construction comes first, in German it usually follows the noun it refers to. Look at the following examples:

Das ist die Tasche *meines Vaters.*	That is *my father's* bag.
Das ist das Auto *meiner Tante.*	That is *my aunt's* car.
Das ist das Spielzeug *meines Babys.*	That is *my baby's* toy.
Das ist die Meinung *meiner Freunde.*	That is *my friends'* opinion.

Like in the accusative and dative cases, the endings of the determiners, for example the indefinite and definite articles, are also affected by the genitive case.

Endings in the genitive case

Here is an overview of the most common determines in the genitive case:

determiners	*masculine*	*feminine*	*neuter*	*plural*
definite	**d*es* Mann*es***	**d*er* Frau**	**d*es* Kind*es***	**d*er* Freunde**
indefinite	**ein*es* Mann*es***	**ein*er* Frau**	**ein*es* Kind*es***	—
possessive	**mein*es* Mann*es***	**mein*er* Frau**	**mein*es* Kind*es***	**mein*er* Freunde**
negative	**kein*es* Mann*es***	**kein*er* Frau**	**kein*es* Kind*es***	**kein*er* Freunde**

As you can see the determiners

- for *masculine* and *neuter* nouns end in **-es**
- for *feminine* and *plural* nouns end in **-er**.

Additional endings for masculine and neuter nouns

Masculine and neuter nouns normally change in the genitive. Most one-syllable nouns add **-es** and longer nouns **-s**:

der Mann → des Mann*es*	**das Auto → des Auto*s***
das Kind → des Kind*es*	**der Computer → des Computer*s***

Nouns in the feminine or the plural do not take an additional ending.

No apostrophe

When an **-s** is added to masculine or neuter nouns, there is no apostrophe in German. The same applies when you refer to a person's name:

Das ist Hannah*s* Scooter.	This is Hannah's scooter.

The genitive case after prepositions

There are also certain prepositions which take the genitive case. The most common are:

trotz	despite
während	during
wegen	because of, due to
(an)statt	instead of

Examples:

Während *seiner* Zeit . . .	During his time . . .
Trotz *ihres* jungen Alters . . .	Despite her young age . . .

It is not very likely that you will use these forms much at the beginners' level. However, it is good to be aware of them.

The genitive case – the main points

The genitive expresses a *possessive relationship* between two nouns. The usage in English and German is very similar, but it is important to remember that the endings for determiners change:

- **-es** for *masculine* and *neuter* nouns and
- **-er** for *feminine* nouns and the *plural.*

Also don't forget – one-syllable neuter and masculine nouns add **-es** and longer ones add **-s**.

Did you know?

In spoken German the genitive is often regarded as too formal and old-fashioned. A common way to replace it is to use **von** + dative:

Der Name seiner Firma ist T+S. → **Der Name *von seiner* Firma ist T+S.**

Das ist das Auto meines Bruders. **Das ist das Auto *von meinem* Bruder.**

- For more information on prepositions see Unit 25.
- For more information on pronouns in the genitive see Unit 16.
- For adjective endings in the genitive see Unit 26.

Exercise 15.1

Replace the genitive construction by using **von** + dative. Make the necessary changes to the determiners and nouns.

Example: Das ist die neue Freundin mein***es*** Bruder**s**.
→ Das ist die neue Freundin ***von*** mein***em*** Bruder.

1 Das ist das Mountainbike meines Sohnes.
2 Das sind die Sportsachen meiner Frau.
3 Das ist das Spielzeug meines Kindes.
4 Das ist die Frau meines Chefs.
5 Da vorne steht der Scooter meiner Schwester.
6 Die Lehrerin meines Englischkurses kommt aus New York.
7 Der Trainer unserer Hockeymannschaft ist sehr gut.
8 Die Meinung meiner Freunde ist mir sehr wichtig.

Exercise 15.2

Fill in the missing endings for the determiners in the genitive case and make the correct changes to the noun, if applicable.

Examples: Wie war der Name dein__ Freund__?
→ Wie war der Name dein***es*** Freund***es***?

Das ist das Auto mein__ Mutter__.
→ Das ist das Auto mein***er*** Mutter.

1 Das ist das Zimmer mein__ Sohn__.
2 Das Cover d__ Buch__ ist sehr attraktiv.
3 Wie war der Name d__ Sängerin__?
4 Der Vorname mein__ Yogalehrerin__ ist Naheeda.
5 Das Hobby mein__ Chefin__ ist Outdoor-Fitness.
6 Der Bildschirm mein__ neuen Tablet__ ist besser für die Augen.
7 Trotz d__ schlechten Wetter__ macht er einen Spaziergang.
8 Während ihr__ Mittagspause__ checkt sie ihre Messages.

Exercise 15.3

Translate the following sentences.

1 That is my brother's scooter.
2 That is my sister's car.
3 These are the friends of my daughter.
4 This is Paula's bag.
5 It was Tim's mistake.

Checklist

1 Which two factors determine the use of the genitive case?
2 What are the determiner endings for masculine and neuter nouns?
3 Can you name the determiner endings for feminine and plural nouns?
4 Which ending will you need to add to masculine and neuter nouns in the genitive?

UNIT 16
Personal pronouns

What are personal pronouns?

A personal pronoun is a word which stands in for a noun, usually for a person or an item:

Sara comes from Melbourne. → *She* comes from Melbourne.

It can also replace a noun group or a whole phrase:

My neighbour's house has been renovated. → *It* has been renovated.

Personal pronouns in German

These are the personal pronouns in German when used as the *subject* in a sentence:

	singular		*plural*	
1st person	**ich**	I	**wir**	we
2nd person	**du**	you (*informal*)	**ihr**	you (*informal*)
	Sie	you (*formal*)	**Sie**	you (*formal*)
3rd person	**er**	he	**sie**	they
	sie	she		
	es	it		

Formal and informal address

As you probably already know, German has different modes for addressing others. You should use

- **du/ihr** for family, friends, children, animals
- **Sie** for people whom you do not know well and who are older than you.

Useful points

Verb endings

The verb endings in German change in accordance with the subject. Here is a short summary of the endings for regular verbs:

ich	***e***	**spiel*e***	**wir**	***en***	**spiel*en***
du	***st***	**spiel*st***	**ihr**	***t***	**spiel*t***
Sie	***en***	**spiel*en***	**Sie**	***en***	**spiel*en***
er/sie/es	***t***	**spiel*t***	**sie**	***en***	**spiel*en***

- For more details of verb endings refer to Units 2–4.

Spelling for 'I' and 'you'

Note that **ich** 'I' in German is spelt with a lower-case letter when it is not at the beginning of a sentence. The formal 'you' **Sie** on the other hand always takes an initial capital letter.

Ja, *ich* wohne in Hamburg. Yes, *I* live in Hamburg.
Sind *Sie* nicht Herr Schweiger? Aren't *you* Mr Schweiger?

Pronouns in German use the grammatical gender

In German, personal pronouns in the third person are used according to grammatical gender. This is different from English, where they are normally used according to 'biological' gender: 'he'/'she' for people and 'it' for things or concepts.

Masculine nouns

Note that masculine nouns are replaced by **er**, regardless of whether they are people, animals or things:

***Der Mann* heißt Daniel.** → ***Er* heißt Daniel.**
***Der Cappuccino* ist gut.** ***Er* ist gut.**

Feminine nouns

Feminine nouns are replaced by **sie**:

***Die Frau* heißt Daniela.** → ***Sie* heißt Daniela.**
***Die Jacke* ist gut.** ***Sie* ist gut.**

Neuter nouns

Neuter nouns are replaced by **es**:

***Das Kind* heißt Jana.**	→	***Es* heißt Jana.**
***Das Passwort* ist gut.**		***Es* ist gut.**

Pronouns change according to case

So far in this unit you have seen how personal pronouns work when they function as the *subject* in a sentence (nominative case). However, personal pronouns can also be the *direct* or the *indirect object*. To show the role the pronoun plays in an English sentence, some of the 'subject' and 'object' pronouns are different: I → me, he → him, she → her, we → us, they → them.

In German, there are also different forms for personal pronouns depending on the role they have in a sentence. However, because of the case system in German there are more pronoun forms than in English.

Pronouns in the accusative case

All forms

Here is a list of the personal pronouns in the accusative case:

	singular		*plural*	
1st person	**mich**	me	**uns**	us
2nd person	**dich**	you (*informal*)	**euch**	you (*informal*)
	Sie	you (*formal*)	**Sie**	you (*formal*)
3rd person	**ihn**	him, it	**sie**	they
	sie	she, it		
	es	it		

Accusative personal pronouns for the direct object

Accusative pronouns are used when they function as the *direct object* in a sentence:

Ich sehe *den Mann.*	→	**Ich sehe *ihn.***
Er kauft *das Auto.*		**Er kauft *es.***
Wir treffen *die Freunde.*		**Wir treffen *sie.***

Here are more examples of accusative personal pronouns in use:

Kennst du *mich*?	Do you know me?
Ich liebe *dich*.	I love you.
Den Rucksack? Ich habe *ihn* gekauft.	The rucksack? I bought it.
Magst du *sie*?	Do you like her?
Er besucht *uns* morgen.	He is going to visit us tomorrow.
Die Sticker. Hast du *sie* gesehen?	The stickers. Have you seen them?

Accusative personal pronouns after prepositions

After prepositions which take the accusative, such as **durch** 'through', **für** 'for', **gegen** 'against, around', **ohne** 'without' and **um** 'around', you'll also need to use the accusative forms:

Ist das *für* ***mich*?**	Is this for me?
Die Blumen sind *für* ***dich*.**	The flowers are for you.
Ohne ***euch*** **möchte ich nicht fahren.**	I wouldn't like to go without you.

Pronouns in the dative case

All forms

Here is a list of personal pronouns in the dative case:

	singular		*plural*	
1st person	**mir**	me	**uns**	us
2nd person	**dir**	you (*informal*)	**euch**	you (*informal*)
	Ihnen	you (*formal*)	**Sie**	you (*formal*)
3rd person	**ihm**	him, it	**sie**	they
	ihr	she, it		
	es	it		

Dative personal pronouns for the indirect object

You need a dative pronoun if it is the *indirect object* in a sentence:

Sie zeigt *dem Mann* das Buch.	→	**Sie zeigt *ihm* das Buch.**
Er schickt *der Frau* eine SMS.		**Er schickt *ihr* eine SMS.**

Sie zeigt *dem Mann* das Buch.	→	**Sie zeigt *ihm* das Buch.**
Sie schenken *den Kindern* Geld.		**Sie schenken *ihnen* Geld.**

Dative personal pronouns after prepositions and verbs

A dative personal pronoun is also required after certain prepositions and verbs.

Prepositions which take the dative case are: **außer** 'apart from', **aus** 'from, out of', **bei** 'at, near', **gegenüber** 'opposite', **mit** 'with', **nach** 'after, to', **seit** 'since, for', **von** 'from' and **zu** 'to'.

Important verbs which require the dative case include **antworten** 'to answer', **danken** 'to thank', **gehören** 'to belong to', **helfen** 'to help' and **folgen** 'to follow'.

Examples:

Sie wohnt bei *mir.*	She lives with me.
Ich kann nicht mit *ihm* arbeiten.	I can't work with him.
Wie komme ich zu *euch*?	How do I get to you?
Er hilft *mir.*	He is helping me.
Gehört das Handy *dir*?	Is this your mobile?
Ich danke *Ihnen.*	I thank you.

The pronoun *man* – 'one, you'

The pronoun **man** 'one, you' is used to refer to people in a general sense. It takes the verb ending of **er/sie/es** and is mainly used in the nominative as the subject of the sentence:

Man tut das nicht.	You don't do that. / One does not do that.
Man darf hier nicht fotografieren.	You are not allowed to take photographs here.

Learning tip

Don't feel overwhelmed by the sheer number of different personal pronouns in German. As a beginner you will mostly use the nominative form (**ich**, **du**, **er**, **sie**, **es** etc.) and some common phrases (**Wie geht es dir?** etc.).

The more exposure you have to the language, the more you will get used to the different forms and the more confident you will feel about dealing with them.

Personal pronouns – summary

Here is an overview of the personal pronouns in German:

	nominative		*accusative*		*dative*	
1st person	**ich**	**wir**	**mich**	**uns**	**mir**	**uns**
2nd person	**du**	**ihr**	**dich**	**euch**	**dir**	**euch**
	Sie	**Sie**	**Sie**	**Sie**	**Ihnen**	**Sie**
3rd person	**er**	**sie**	**ihn**	**sie**	**ihm**	**sie**
	sie		**sie**		**ihr**	
	es		**es**		**es**	

Did you know?

Dative pronouns are used in a number of frequently used expressions in German:

Wie geht es dir/Ihnen/euch?	How are you?
Es geht mir gut.	I am well.
Es tut mir leid.	I am sorry.
Meine Nase/Mein Bein tut mir weh.	My nose/My leg hurts.
Mir ist kalt/heiß.	I am cold/hot.
Gefällt dir/Ihnen das T-Shirt?	Do you like the T-shirt?
Können Sie mir sagen, wieviel Uhr es ist?	Can you tell me what time it is?

Exercise 16.1

Replace the subject of each sentence with a personal pronoun.

Example: *Carla* hat eine Schwester. → ***Sie*** hat eine Schwester.

1. *Oliver* kommt aus Bremen.
2. *Angela* hat einen neuen Freund.
3. *Das Fahrrad* ist neu.
4. *Die Kinder* spielen im Park Fußball.
5. *Die Blumen* waren teuer.
6. *Die Pizza* kostet 7.50 Euro.
7. *Die Mannschaft* hat einen schlechten Tag.
8. *Das Kind* heißt Lena.
9. *Mein Onkel* ist Ingenieur von Beruf.
10. *Meine Kollegen* machen Urlaub in einem Wellnesshotel.

Exercise 16.2

Answer each of the following questions with 'yes', using the appropriate accusative personal pronoun in your response.

Example: Kaufst du *das Internetradio*? → Ja, ich kaufe ***es***.

1. Kaufst du das Smartphone?
2. Kennst du den Mann?
3. Kennst du die Schauspielerin?
4. Hast du das Geld?
5. Trinkst du den Caffè macchiato?
6. Möchtest du die Pralinen?
7. Magst du die Leute?
8. Besuchst du mich?
9. Besuchst du uns?
10. Geht es dir gut?

Exercise 16.3

Supply the correct dative pronoun from the list below. The first one has been done.

ihnen ihnen dir ~~ihr~~ ihm uns mir euch mir Ihnen

1	Schenkst du Tina etwas?	– Ja, ich schenke *ihr* Blumen.
2	Gefällt dir die Party?	– Nein, die Party gefällt ____ überhaupt nicht.
3	Kaufst du Matthias ein T-Shirt?	– Nein, ich kaufe ____ eine Baseballmütze.
4	Hilfst du den Kindern?	– Ja, ich helfe ____.
5	Kannst du mir helfen?	– Ja, ich helfe ____.
6	Können Sie mir helfen?	– Ja, ich helfe ____.
7	Gehört das Ihnen?	– Ja, es gehört ____.
8	Was bringst du denn Anna und Tina mit?	– Ich kaufe ____ eine Flasche Biowein.
9	Soll ich euch die Wohnung zeigen?	– Ja, zeig sie ____, bitte.
10	Schickst du uns ein Selfie aus dem Urlaub?	– Ja, ich schicke ____ ein Selfie.

Exercise 16.4

Translate the following sentences.

1. The coffee is good. It is good.
2. The jacket is new. It is new.

3 Is this for me?
4 I am buying him a bottle of wine.
5 He sends her a text message.
6 How are you? (Use the **du** and **Sie** forms for 'you'.)
7 I am very well.
8 I am sorry.

Checklist

1 Do you know when to use the formal and informal modes of address?
2 What is meant by grammatical gender? Why is it important for personal pronouns?
3 Do you know all the personal pronouns in the accusative case?
4 Do you know all the personal pronouns in the dative case?
5 Can you name three frequently used expressions with a dative personal pronoun?

UNIT 17

Possessive adjectives

What are possessive adjectives?

Possessives are words such as 'my', 'your', 'his', 'her' which indicate that something belongs to somebody.

Usage in English and German

Possessives are used in a similar way in English and in German. If something belongs to a male person, use 'his' to indicate that it belongs to him. If something belongs to a female or to more than one person, you choose 'her' or a plural form such as 'our' or 'their'.

***sein* Haus**	his house
***ihr* Auto**	her car
***unsere* Tochter**	our daughter
***ihre* Kinder**	their children

The possessive adjectives in German

Here is an overview of the possessive adjectives:

singular				*plural*			
ich	→	**mein**	my	**wir**	→	**unser**	our
du		**dein**	your	**ihr**		**euer**	your
Sie		**Ihr**	your	**Sie**		**Ihr**	your
er		**sein**	his	**sie**		**ihr**	their
sie		**ihr**	her				
es		**sein**	his				

Possessive adjectives require endings

In German, the endings of possessive adjectives must agree in gender, number and case with the noun that they are linked to. However, this is not as complicated as it sounds. The endings follow the pattern of the indefinite article **ein**, with some variations in the plural.

Possessive adjective endings in the nominative case

In the nominative case, there are no possessive adjective endings before masculine and neuter nouns. If the noun is feminine or plural, **-e** is added to the possessive:

Das ist mein Bruder.	This is my brother.
Das ist mein*e* Mutter.	This is my mother.
Das ist mein Auto.	This is my car.
Mein*e* Geschwister wohnen in Berlin.	My brothers and sisters live in Berlin.

Possessive adjective endings in the accusative case

You probably remember the change in the accusative case, where the indefinite article for masculine nouns changes from **ein** to **ein*en***. Possessive adjectives follow the same pattern and add **-en** when they appear before a masculine noun. The feminine and plural forms take an extra **-e**.

Sie trifft ihr*en* Bruder.	She meets her brother.
Sie trifft ihr*e* Schwester.	She meets her sister.
Sie sieht ihr Kind.	She sees her child.
Sie trifft ihr*e* Freunde.	She meets her friends.

Possessive adjective endings in the dative case

In the dative case, the possessive takes the endings **-em** when referring to masculine and neuter nouns and **-er** if the noun is feminine. In the plural **-en** is added:

Er spricht mit sein*em* Bruder.	He talks to his brother.
Er spricht mit sein*er* Schwester.	He talks to his sister.
Er spricht mit sein*em* Kind.	He talks to his child.
Er spricht mit sein*en* Eltern.	He talks to his parents.

Possessive adjective endings in the genitive case

At the beginners' level you are unlikely to use possessives in the genitive case, but you may encounter them in a written or in other media. They have **-es** endings for masculine and neuter and add **-er** for feminine nouns and the plural:

Das ist der Freund unser*es* Sohnes. This is the friend of our son.
Das ist der Freund unser*er* Tochter. This is the friend of our daughter.
Das ist der Freund unser*es* Kindes. This is the friend of our child.
Die Freunde unser*er* Kinder sind sehr nett. The friends of our children are very nice.

Spelling variation for **euer**

Note that **euer** ('your', informal plural) drops the second **e** when any ending is added, for example in connection with a feminine or plural noun:

Ist das *eure* Mutter? Is that your mother?
Sind das *eure* Eltern? Are these your parents?

Summary of possessive adjective endings

Here is an overview of the endings for the possessive adjectives:

	masculine	*feminine*	*neuter*	*plural*
nominative	**mein Mann**	**mein*e* Frau**	**mein Baby**	**mein*e* Kinder**
accusative	**mein*en* Mann**	**mein*e* Frau**	**mein Baby**	**mein*e* Kinder**
dative	**mein*em* Mann**	**mein*er* Frau**	**mein*em* Baby**	**mein*en* Kindern**
genitive	**mein*es* Mannes**	**mein*er* Frau**	**mein*es* Babys**	**mein*er* Kinder**

Did you know?

Ihr/ihr can have four meanings: 'her', 'their' and 'your' in the formal singular and formal plural. However, the context will normally make it clear what **ihr** or **Ihr** refers to. In writing, it helps that the two formal 'your' forms always start with a capital.

- For more information on how cases work and on endings for the accusative, dative and genitive cases see Units 11–15.

Exercise 17.1

Match up the English possessives with their German equivalents from the list. The first one has been done.

sein ihr Ihr euer dein unser sein ~~mein~~ Ihr ihr

my	**mein**	our	_____
your (*singular, informal*)	_____	your (*plural, informal*)	_____
your (*singular, formal*)	_____	your (*plural, formal*)	_____
his	_____	their	_____
her	_____		
its	_____		

Exercise 17.2

Fill in the missing endings in the nominative case. Sometimes no endings are needed.

Example: Wie ist Ihr__ Adresse? – Mein__ Adresse ist Falkenweg 12.
→ Wie ist Ihr*e* Adresse? – Mein*e* Adresse ist Falkenweg 12.

1 Wie ist dein__ Name? – Mein__ Name ist Frank Auerbach.
2 Wie ist dein__ Telefonnummer? – Mein__ Telefonnummer ist 863001.
3 Ist das sein__ Auto? – Nein, das ist ihr__ Auto.
4 Was sind Ihr__ Hobbys? – Mein__ Hobbys sind Joggen und Skifahren.
5 Was sind eu__ Namen? – Unser__ Namen sind Svenja und Boris.
6 Sind das eu__ Sportsachen? – Ja, das sind unser__ Sportsachen.

Exercise 17.3

Write sentences describing what these people are looking for, following the two examples. Use the accusative case.

Examples: Max → Führerschein (*m*) → Max sucht ***seinen*** Führerschein.
Claudia → Tasche (*f*) → Claudia sucht ***ihre*** Tasche.

1 Tom → Brille (*f*) __________
2 Paula → Geld (*nt*) __________
3 Mehmet → Controller (*m*) __________
4 Marion → Schal (*m*) __________
5 Martha → SIM-Karte (*f*) __________
6 Benjamin → I-Pad (*nt*) __________
7 Peter → Schuhe (*pl*) __________
8 Jessica und Pia → Pässe (*pl*) __________

Exercise 17.4

Translate the following sentences.

1 This is my father.
2 This is my mother.

3 Marc is looking for his SIM card.
4 Susanne is looking for her driving licence.
5 We meet our friends.
6 Sebastian talks to his mother.
7 Arianne talks to her brother.
8 The children talk to their grandparents.

Checklist

1 Can you name all the possessive adjectives in German?
2 What do the endings of the possessives have to agree with?
3 Which possessive adjective changes its spelling when it is for instance used with a feminine or plural noun?
4 What can **Ihr/ihr** refer to?

UNIT 18
Reflexive verbs

What are reflexive verbs?

Reflexive verbs refer to an action that a person is doing to himself or herself. Examples in English are: 'I cut myself.' 'He enjoys himself immensely.'

Frequency of use

Reflexive verbs are more frequent in German than in English. They often refer to daily activities, so they are very useful when you want to talk, for instance, about your daily routine.

Important reflexive verbs

Here are some frequently used reflexive verbs in German:

sich amüsieren	to enjoy oneself
sich anziehen	to get dressed
sich ärgern	to get, to be annoyed
sich ausziehen	to get undressed
sich bedanken	to say thank you
sich beeilen	to hurry (up)
sich duschen	to shower oneself/to have a shower
sich entscheiden	to decide
sich entschuldigen	to apologise
sich kämmen	to comb one's hair
sich rasieren	to shave
sich schminken	to put make-up on
sich setzen	to sit down
sich treffen	to meet, to meet (up)
sich umziehen	to get changed
sich unterhalten	to talk, chat
sich verabschieden	to say goodbye

sich vorstellen	to introduce oneself
sich waschen	to wash oneself/to have a wash

Reflexive pronouns – accusative

A reflexive verb is always accompanied by a so-called *reflexive pronoun*, a word such as 'myself', 'yourself' or 'himself'. Most reflexive verbs simply take the *accusative* pronouns: **mich**, **dich**, **sich**, **uns**, **euch** and **sich**. Here is how they go with **sich waschen** 'to have a wash':

Ich wasche *mich*.	**Wir waschen *uns*.**
Du wäschst *dich*.	**Ihr wascht *euch*.**
Sie waschen *sich*.	**Sie waschen *sich*.**
Er/Sie/Es wäscht *sich*.	**Sie waschen *sich*.**

Here are more examples of reflexive verbs with accusative pronouns:

Ich beeile *mich*.	I hurry (up).
Duschen Sie *sich* jeden Tag?	Do you have a shower every day?
Können Sie *sich* vorstellen?	Can you introduce yourself?
Er rasiert *sich*.	He shaves (himself).
Maja kämmt *sich*.	Maja combs her hair.
Wir treffen *uns* mit Steffi.	We meet up with Steffi.
Amüsiert ihr *euch*?	Are you enjoying yourself?
Sie unterhalten *sich* über Musik.	They talk about music.

When to use a dative pronoun

Reflexive verbs usually take the accusative pronoun. A change occurs sometimes when you want to add, for instance, what clothes you are putting on or what part of the body you are cleaning:

Ich ziehe mich an.	→	**Ich ziehe *mir* eine Jacke an.**	I put on a jacket.
Ich wasche mich.		**Ich wasche *mir* die Haare**.	I wash my hair.

With this kind of structure the new item becomes the direct object of the sentence, and the reflexive pronoun – as the indirect object – takes the dative form. There are also some reflexive verbs that only take a dative pronoun, such as **sich überlegen** 'to think something over', **sich vornehmen** 'to intend to do'.

Here is an overview of all reflexive dative pronouns:

Ich wasche *mir* die Haare.	**Wir waschen *uns* die Haare.**
Du wäschst *dir* die Haare.	**Ihr wascht *euch* die Haare.**
Sie waschen *sich* die Haare.	**Sie waschen *sich* die Haare.**
Er/Sie/Es wäscht *sich* die Haare.	**Sie waschen *sich* die Haare.**

Note that **sich** is the same in the dative as in the accusative. This also applies to **uns** and **euch**. The only two pronoun forms that differ from the accusative are **mir** and **dir**.

Separable verbs

When a reflexive verb is separable, the pronoun tends to follow the verb and the prefix goes to the end of the sentence or main clause:

anziehen	→	**Ich ziehe mich *an*.**	I get dressed.
vorstellen		**Er stellt sich dem Publikum *vor*.**	He introduces himself to the audience.

Reflexive and non-reflexive verbs

Most reflexive verbs in German can also be used in a non-reflexive way:

Ich wasche das Auto. (*non-reflexive*)
Ich wasche mich. (*reflexive*)

However, there are some verbs, such as **sich beeilen** and **sich bedanken**, which can only be used as a reflexive verb.

Useful expressions

Note the following commonly used expressions involving reflexive verbs:

Wasch dir die Hände!	Wash your hands.
Ich putze mir die Zähne.	I brush my teeth.
Er putzt sich die Nase.	He blows his nose.
Sie schminkt sich.	She puts on her make-up.

Did you know?

The verb **treffen** can be used as a reflexive or a non-reflexive verb when talking about meeting someone. Used reflexively, it appears with **mit**, which is followed by the dative, whereas the non-reflexive version requires the accusative:

Ich treffe meine Schwester. (*non-reflexive*)
Ich treffe meine Freunde.
Ich treffe mich mit mein*er* Schwester. (*reflexive*)
Ich treffe mich mit mein*en* Freunde*n*.

- For pronouns see Unit 16.
- For more information on the accusative case see Unit 13.
- For more details on the dative case see Unit 14.

Exercise 18.1

Which of these verbs are reflexive? Put a tick in the relevant box. The first one has been done.

amüsieren	✓	beeilen		entscheiden		einkaufen	
anziehen		studieren		entschuldigen		tanzen	
ausgehen		duschen		fahren		unterhalten	
ausziehen		arbeiten		kämmen		waschen	

Exercise 18.2

Make complete sentences using the information given.

Example: er / sich bedanken / für das Geschenk
→ Er bedankt sich für das Geschenk.

1 er / sich entschuldigen / bei seiner Freundin
2 das Kind / sich kämmen / nicht gern
3 ich / sich ärgern / über die Preise
4 ich / sich umziehen
5 Anne / sich anziehen / ihr neues Kleid
6 die Kinder / sich waschen
7 die Spieler / sich duschen / nach dem Spiel
8 wir / sich beeilen
9 wir / sich treffen / um acht Uhr
10 wir / sich verabschieden

Exercise 18.3

Supply the reflexive pronoun in the dative.

Example: Er putzt ____ die Nase. → Er putzt ***sich*** die Nase.

1 Ich wasche ____ die Hände.
2 Putzt du ____ heute nicht die Zähne?
3 Zieh ____ etwas Warmes an. Es ist kalt.
4 Ich wasche ____ das Gesicht nur mit Wasser.

Exercise 18.4

Daily routine. Translate the following sentences.

1 I have a shower.
2 I brush my teeth.
3 I get dressed.
4 I comb my hair.
5 I put on a jacket.
6 I hurry up.

Checklist

1 What are reflexive verbs always accompanied by?
2 What do many commonly used reflexive verbs refer to?
3 Which case do most reflexive pronouns take?
4 Do you know two sentences with a dative reflexive pronoun?

UNIT 19
Negatives

Negative statements

There are different ways to make a negative statement, depending on whether you are dealing with an adjective, a verb or a noun.

Negatives in English

In English, you normally use 'not' or 'do not' with adjectives and verbs:

The blog is not interesting.
They do not (don't) drink coffee.

With nouns, negations can take various forms, such as 'no', 'do not' or 'not any':

There are *no* vegetables left.
He *doesn't have* children.
I *haven't got any* money.

Negatives in German

German uses two main words to give a sentence a negative meaning: **nicht** and **kein**.

- **Nicht** is normally used in connection with *adjectives* and *verbs*:

Das Wetter ist gut. The weather is fine.	→	**Das Wetter ist *nicht* gut.** The weather is not good.
Ich arbeite. I work.	→	**Ich arbeite *nicht*.** I don't work.

- **Kein** is normally linked to nouns:

Ich habe ein Auto.	→	**Ich habe *kein* Auto.**
I've got a car.		I haven't got a car.

Here are the forms in more detail.

Nicht in detail

Nicht corresponds to the English 'not'. It is used in connection with an adjective or a verb:

Nicht + *adjective*

Die Smartwatch ist *nicht* teuer.	The smartwatch is not expensive.
Das Hotel ist *nicht* schön.	The hotel is not beautiful.

Nicht + *verb*

Ich verstehe *nicht*.	I don't understand.
Sie kommt *nicht*.	She isn't coming.

Position of **nicht**

Nicht can appear in various positions in a sentence. The following guidelines may help you when using **nicht** at beginners' level:

- In the present tense **nicht** usually follows the verb:

  Sie jobbt *nicht*.
  Ich fahre *nicht* mit der U-Bahn.

- It tends to go between a verb and **gern**:

  Sie isst *nicht* gern Sushi.

- **Nicht** may be preceded by an expression of time:

  Sie kommt heute *nicht*.

- When used with reflexive verbs, **nicht** is normally placed after the reflexive pronoun:

  Ich entschuldige mich *nicht*.

- In the present perfect tense formed with **haben**, **nicht** often goes just before the past participle:

  Ich habe den Haartrockner *nicht* gekauft.

- However, in the present perfect tense formed with **sein**, **nicht** tends to appear earlier in the sentence:

  Ich bin *nicht* ins Kino gegangen.

Kein in detail

The other important word in German that gives a sentence a negative meaning is **kein**, which is normally linked to a noun:

***Kein* Problem.**	No problem.
Das ist *keine* Antwort.	This is not an answer.
Ich habe *keine* Zeit.	I don't have any time.

Note that **kein** corresponds to 'no', 'not a(n)', 'not any' or 'do not have'/'haven't got' in English.

Endings for ***kein***

Kein is the negative form of **ein** and must therefore also agree with the noun in gender (*masculine*, *feminine*, *neuter*), number (*singular*, *plural*) and case:

Er hat *keinen* Bruder. (*accusative*, *masculine*)
Sie hat *keine* Schwester. (*accusative*, *feminine*)
Er hat *kein* Kind. (*accusative*, *neuter*)
Sie hat *keine* Geschwister. (*accusative*, *plural*)

Here is an overview of all endings for **kein**:

	masculine	*feminine*	*neuter*	*plural*
nominative	**kein Mann**	**kein*e* Frau**	**kein Baby**	**kein*e* Kinder**
accusative	**kein*en* Mann**	**kein*e* Frau**	**kein Baby**	**kein*e* Kinder**
dative	**kein*em* Mann**	**kein*er* Frau**	**kein*em* Baby**	**kein*en* Kindern**
genitive	**kein*es* Mannes**	**kein*er* Frau**	**kein*es* Babys**	**kein*er* Kindern**

As you can see, the endings are identical with the endings for **ein**, except for the plural, where they follow the endings for the possessive adjectives, such as **mein**, **dein**.

Examples of ***kein*** *in use*

Here are some examples of **kein** in the nominative:

Das ist ein schlechter Film.	→	**Das ist *kein* schlechter Film.**
Das ist *eine* gute Idee.	→	**Das ist *keine* gute Idee.**
Das ist *ein* Spiel für Kinder.	→	**Das ist *kein* Spiel für Kinder.**

Kein also appears in a number of frequently used expressions:

Sie hat keine Geduld.	She doesn't have any patience.
Ich habe kein Glück.	I am unlucky.
Ich habe kein Geld.	I don't have money. / I haven't got money.

Phrases where *nicht* or *kein* can be used

With some expressions you can use either **nicht** or **kein**. They include:

Ich spreche nicht/kein Deutsch.	I don't speak German.
Er ist nicht/kein Ingenieur.	He isn't an engineer.

Did you know?

If you want to say 'but' after a negative statement in order to give a corrected version, you normally use **sondern** in German, instead of **aber**:

Er wohnt nicht Berlin, sondern in Bremen.	He doesn't live in Berlin but in Bremen.
Sie ist keine Ärztin, sondern Physiotherapeutin.	She isn't a doctor but a physiotherapist.
Ich zahle nicht bar, sondern mit Karte.	I'm not paying cash, but by card.

Exercise 19.1

Change the sentences below into the negative using **nicht**. Make sure you put **nicht** in the appropriate position.

Example: Peter arbeitet. → Peter arbeitet ***nicht***.

1 Franziska joggt.
2 Mario ist clever.
3 Der Film ist interessant.
4 Das Wetter in England ist gut.
5 Er fotografiert gern.
6 Nadine macht gern Outdoorsport.
7 Er fährt gern mit seinem Mountainbike.
8 Monica kommt aus Österreich.
9 Er ist verheiratet.
10 Mia studiert Medizin.
11 Sie geht heute ins Konzert.
12 Er spielt gut Klavier.

13 Ich habe die App gekauft.
14 Er hat die E-Mail gelesen.

Exercise 19.2

Fill in the correct form of **kein** from the list below. The first one has been done.

keine ~~kein~~ kein keinen kein kein keine

1 Das Team hat ***kein*** Glück.
2 Sie hat ___ Geduld.
3 Er hat im Moment ___ Geld.
4 Elena hat ___ Bruder.
5 Ich habe ___ Zeit.
6 Das ist ___ Problem.
7 Er ist Veganer und isst ___ Fleisch.

Exercise 19.3

Give a negative response to all questions by using the correct form of **kein**.

Example: Ist das ein Porsche? → Nein, das ist ***kein*** Porsche.

1 Ist das ein Park?
2 Ist das eine Kneipe?
3 Hast du ein Auto?
4 Möchtest du einen Kaffee?
5 Nimmst du einen Nachtisch?
6 Hat Alina eine Schwester?
7 Hat das Hotel einen Wellnessbereich?
8 Haben Sie Geschwister?
9 Haben Sie Wanderschuhe?
10 Hat Freiburg eine U-Bahn?
11 Hat Julian Geld?
12 Hast du Zeit?

Exercise 19.4

Challenge yourself. Translate the following sentences.

1 Luke doesn't work.
2 The hotel is not beautiful.
3 The tablet is not cheap.

4 Paul doesn't have a mountain bike.
5 They don't have a car.
6 This is not a good idea.
7 He hasn't got any time.
8 She doesn't live in London, but in New York.
9 I don't drink coffee, but tea.
10 This is not a problem.

Checklist

1 With what kind of words do you use **nicht** to give a sentence a negative meaning?
2 When do you normally use **kein**?
3 How does **kein** have to agree with the noun?
4 What word do you often use instead of **aber** after a negative statement?

UNIT 20

Comparison of adjectives and adverbs

Comparative and superlative

When you make comparisons, you can state that some items are smaller, bigger, cheaper, more expensive etc. (*comparative*) or that one is the smallest, the biggest etc. (*superlative*).

Usage in English

In English, the comparative is formed by adding '-er' to short adjectives or by using the word 'more':

This laptop is cheap*er*.
London is much *more* interesting than Paris.

To form the superlative you either use 'the' and add the '-est' or use the words 'the most':

This laptop is *the* cheap*est*.
London is *the most* interesting city.

Formation in German

In German, the *comparative* is formed by adding **-er** to the basic form, regardless of how long the adjective is:

billig → **Dieser Laptop ist billig*er*.**
interessant → **London ist viel interessant*er* als Paris.**

For the *superlative*, add **-sten** to the adjective and put **am** before it, if the superlative comes after the noun:

billig → **Dieser Laptop ist *am* billig*sten*.**

Here are all forms in more detail.

The comparative adjective in more detail

Adding -er

Most adjectives simply add **-er** in the comparative:

klein	small	→	**klein*er***	smaller
cool	cool, trendy		**cool*er***	cooler, more trendy
schnell	fast		**schnell*er***	faster
hässlich	ugly		**hässlich*er***	uglier
langweilig	boring		**langweilig*er***	more boring
ökologisch	ecological		**ökologisch*er***	more ecological

Adding umlaut + -er

Most short adjectives with the stem vowel **a**, **o** or **u** also add an umlaut. Here are some examples:

alt	old	→	***ä*lt*er***	older
arm	poor		***ä*rm*er***	poorer
jung	young		**j*ü*ng*er***	younger
groß	big, tall		**gr*ö*ß*er***	bigger, taller
kalt	cold		**k*ä*lt*er***	colder
lang	long		**l*ä*ng*er***	longer
stark	strong		**st*ä*rk*er***	stronger
warm	warm		**w*ä*rm*er***	warmer

Monosyllabic adjectives which do not take an umlaut include **flach** 'flat' → **flacher** 'flatter', **klar** 'clear' → **klarer** 'clearer' and **voll** 'full' → **voller** 'fuller'.

Note that **gesund**, which consists of two syllable, also adds an umlaut: **gesund** 'healthy' → **gesünder** 'healthier'.

Irregular forms

Most adjectives follow a regular pattern. There are only a few exceptions. The most important one is:

gut	good	→	**besser**	better

Note also the spelling variations for:

hoch	high	→	**höher**	higher

To make them easier to pronounce, adjectives ending in **-er** and **-el** drop the **e** in the comparative:

teuer	expensive	→	**teurer**	more expensive
dunkel	dark		**dunkler**	darker

How to say 'than'

The German equivalent of 'than' is **als**:

Berlin ist größer *als* München.	Berlin is bigger than Munich.
Der Rhein ist länger *als* die Donau.	The Rhine is longer than the Danube.

The superlative adjective in more detail

Adding ***-sten***

The superlative is formed by adding **-sten** to the adjective. In addition, it is preceded by the word **am**:

klein	small	→	***am* klein*sten***	(the) smallest
cool	cool, trendy		***am* cool*sten***	(the) coolest
schnell	fast		***am* schnell*sten***	(the) fastest
hässlich	ugly		***am* hässlich*sten***	(the) ugliest
langweilig	boring		***am* langweilig*sten***	(the) most boring
ökologisch	ecological		***am* ökologisch*sten***	(the) most ecological

Adding umlaut + ***-sten***

As in the comparative form, most monosyllabic adjectives with stem vowel **a**, **o** or **u** add an umlaut, including:

jung	young	→	***am* jüng*sten***	(the) youngest
groß	big, tall		***am* größ*ten***	(the) biggest, tallest
lang	long		***am* läng*sten***	(the) longest
warm	warm		***am* wärm*sten***	(the) warmest

There are some exceptions such as **flach** 'flat' → **am flachsten** '(the) flattest', **klar** 'clear' → **am klarsten** '(the) clearest' and **voll** 'full' → **am vollsten** '(the) fullest'.
Note that **größten** only adds **–ten** and not **–sten**.

Irregular forms

Adjectives which do not follow a regular pattern include:

gut	good	→	**am besten**	(the) best

There is a spelling variation for **nah** 'close', while the superlative for **hoch** 'high' is regular:

am nächsten	(the) closest
am höchsten	(the) highest

Adjectives ending in **-er** and **-el** which drop the **e** in the comparative 'retake' it in the superlative:

teuer	expensive	→	**am teuersten**	(the) most expensive
dunkel	dark		**am dunkelsten**	(the) darkest

Adjectives ending in ***-d, -t, -s, -z***

To make pronunciation easier, adjectives ending in **-d**, **-t**, **-s**, **-z** usually add an extra **e** before **-sten** in the superlative:

kalt	cold	→	**am kält*esten***	(the) coldest
kurz	short		**am kürz*esten***	(the) shortest
gesund	healthy		**am gesünd*esten***	(the) healthiest
interessant	interesting		**am interessant*esten***	(the) most interesting

Comparative and superlative of adverbs

Adverbs are used with verbs

While adjectives provide more information about nouns, adverbs give additional information about verbs:

adjective	*adverb*
Sie ist schön. She is beautiful.	**Sie tanzt sehr schön.** She dances beautifully.

Adverbs in German

In English, adverbs usually have a different form from adjectives – in most cases you add '-ly' ('beautiful' → 'beautifully'). In German, most adverbs have the same form as adjectives.

Using adverbs in the comparative and superlative

The comparative and superlative of adverbs therefore work in exactly the same way and follow all the rules described above for adjectives. Here are some examples of adverbs in use:

Jana läuft langsam.	→	**Kira läuft langsam*er*.**	→	**Paula läuft *am* langsam*sten*.**
Jana runs slowly.		Kira runs slower.		Paula runs the slowest.

Timo singt schlecht. →	**Sascha singt schlecht*er*.** →	**Jan singt *am* schlecht*esten*.**
Timo sings badly.	Sascha sings worse.	Jan sings the worst.
Das Hardcover kostet wenig. →	**Das Paperback kostet wenig*er*.** →	**Das E-Book kostet *am* wenig*sten*.**
The hardcover costs little.	The paperback costs less.	The e-book costs the least.

Using ***gern*** *and* ***viel***

Gern 'like' and **viel** 'a lot' are two frequently used adverbs. Both follow an irregular pattern:

Ich trinke *gern* Wasser. →	**Ich trinke *lieber* Kaffee.** →	**Ich trinke *am liebsten* Bier.**
I like drinking water.	I prefer drinking coffee.	I like drinking beer best of all.
Björn twittert *viel*. →	**Rania twittert *mehr*.** →	**Axel twittert *am meisten*.**
Björn tweets a lot.	Rania tweets more.	Axel tweets the most.

Using comparatives and superlatives before nouns

The examples in this unit relate to comparative and superlative forms *following* nouns. These forms may change endings when they appear *before* a noun. See Unit 26 for more information.

Did you know?

There is another way of making comparisons in German. If you compare two items which imply equality, use **so … wie** 'as … as':

Es ist so kalt wie gestern.	It is as cold as yesterday.
Er ist so groß wie sein Bruder.	He is as tall as his brother.
Der Film ist so gut wie das Buch.	The film is as good as the book.

Exercise 20.1

Fill in the missing forms of the adjectives or adverbs below. The first one has been done.

	comparative	*superlative*
klein	**klein*er***	***am* klein*sten***
	langweilig*er*	
alt		
groß		
		am höch*sten*
	interessant*er*	
intelligent		
umweltfreundlich		
		am be*sten*
gern		
	mehr	

Exercise 20.2

Put the words in brackets in the appropriate comparative or superlative form.

Example: Patrick ist ___ als Susanna. (jung)
→ Patrick ist ***jünger*** als Susanna.

1 Ist der Rhein wirklich ____ als die Donau? (lang)
2 Norddeutschland ist ____ als Süddeutschland. (flach)
3 Der Zug ist ____ als das Flugzeug. (billig)
4 Ist das I-Pad ____ als das I-Phone? (teuer)
5 Ich finde das Buch ____ als den Film. (interessant)
6 Die neue Castingshow ist ____ als die alte. (langweilig)
7 Auf dem Land ist es ____ als in der Stadt. (ruhig)
8 Heute ist es ____ als gestern. (kalt)
9 Das neue Modell ist ____. (ökologisch)
10 Er lebt jetzt ____ als früher. (gesund)
11 Welcher Berg in Österreich ist am ____? (hoch)
12 Welche Musik hörst du am ____? (gern)
13 Welches Auto ist am ____? (umweltfreundlich)
14 Dieser Club ist im Moment am ____. (cool)
15 Diese Pizza schmeckt am ___. (gut)

Exercise 20.3

Make comparisons by following the example.

Example: Im Frühling ist es warm. – im Herbst / im Sommer
→ Im Herbst ist es wärmer. Im Sommer ist es am wärmsten.

1 München ist groß. – Hamburg / Berlin
2 Die Donau ist lang. – die Elbe / der Rhein
3 Salat schmeckt gut. – Pasta / Pizza
4 Tim spricht klar. – Jan / Anna
5 Susanne macht viel Sport. – Nele / Anke
6 Ich trinke gern Kaffee. – grünen Tee / schwarzen Tee
7 Portugiesisch ist kompliziert. – Ungarisch / Chinesisch
8 Frankfurt ist multikulturell. – Hamburg / Berlin

Exercise 20.4

Translate the following sentences.

1 London is bigger than Paris.
2 The Rhine is longer than the Danube.
3 Jan is older than Gabriel.
4 Boris is more intelligent than Moritz.
5 Hannah is the most intelligent.
6 The train is more ecological than the plane.
7 The book is better than the film.
8 Tim is as tall as his brother.
9 This pizza tastes the best.

Checklist

1 How is the comparative formed?
2 How is the superlative formed?
3 Is there a different form for the comparative or superlative of long adjectives or adverbs?
4 When is there often a change in the stem of the adjective or adverb?
5 What changes are sometimes introduced to make pronunciation easier?

UNIT 21
Modal verbs

What are modal verbs?

Modals are verbs which express a certain 'mood' in a sentence; for example you *can* do something, *should* do something or *must* do something.

The six modal verbs in German

There are the six modal verbs in German:

dürfen	may, to be allowed to
können	can, to be able to
müssen	must, to have to
sollen	should, to be supposed to, ought to
wollen	to want to
mögen	to like

All modal verbs are quite irregular and often have a stem vowel change in the present tense.

Modal verbs in detail

Dürfen 'may, to be allowed to'

The modal **dürfen** is used to express permission:

Sie *dürfen* hier parken.	You are allowed to park here.

When used in a question it adds a sense of politeness and corresponds to the English 'may'.

***Darf* ich Ihnen helfen?**	May I help you?

It is highly irregular and has a vowel change in the **ich**, **du** and **er/sie/es** forms. Note that **ich** and **er/sie/es** also do not have the **-e** and **-t** endings:

ich darf	**wir dürfen**
du darfst	**ihr dürft**
Sie dürfen	**Sie dürfen**
er/sie/es darf	**sie dürfen**

When used with **nicht**, **dürfen** conveys the meaning of something you/one *must not* do:

Sie *dürfen* hier *nicht* parken.	You must not park here.
Man *darf* hier *nicht* fotografieren.	You are not allowed to take photographs here.

Können 'can, to be able to'

The modal **können** means 'can' or 'to be able to':

***Kannst* du mir helfen?**	Can you help me?
Er *kann* sehr gut kochen.	He can cook very well.

Können follows a similar pattern to **dürfen**: there is a vowel change in the **ich**, **du** and **er/sie/es** forms, and **ich** and **er/sie/es** do not have their usual endings:

ich kann	**wir können**
du kannst	**ihr könnt**
Sie können	**Sie können**
er/sie/es kann	**sie können**

Müssen 'must, to have to'

The modal **müssen** means 'must' or 'to have to' in English:

Ich *muss* jetzt gehen.	I must/have to go now.
Er *muss* morgen arbeiten.	He must/has to work tomorrow.

When used with the negative **nicht**, **müssen** does not convey the meaning of prohibition, as in English, but means 'don't have to': are not obliged to

Du *musst nicht* gehen.	You don't have to go.
Du *musst* dich *nicht* entschuldigen.	You don't have to apologise.

To say 'you must not'/'you are not allowed to', use **dürfen** + **nicht** or **kein**:

Sie dürfen hier keine Selfies machen.	You are not allowed to take any selfies here.
Hier dürfen Sie nicht rauchen.	You must not smoke here.

Note also that **müssen** drops its umlaut for the **ich**, **du** and **er/sie/es** forms. Also, **ich** and **er/sie/es** do not have their usual verb endings:

ich muss	**wir müssen**
du musst	**ihr müsst**
Sie müssen	**Sie müssen**
er/sie/es muss	**sie müssen**

Sollen *'to be supposed to, should, ought to'*

The modal **sollen** means 'to be supposed to' or 'should':

Sie *sollen* mehr Sport machen.	You should do more sport.
Was *soll* das bedeuten?	What is this supposed to mean?

There are no vowel changes for **sollen**, but the **ich** and **er/sie/es** forms drop their endings:

ich soll	**wir sollen**
du sollst	**ihr sollt**
Sie sollen	**Sie sollen**
er/sie/es soll	**sie sollen**

Wollen *'to want to'*

The modal **wollen** usually expresses an intention or desire and corresponds to the English 'to want to':

Ich *will* nach New York fliegen.	I want to fly to New York.
Sie *will* etwas essen.	She wants to eat something.

This modal has a vowel change and no endings in the **ich**, **du** and **er/sie/es** forms:

ich will	**wir wollen**
du willst	**ihr wollt**
Sie wollen	**Sie wollen**
er/sie/es will	**sie wollen**

Note that **wollen** cannot be used in the sense of the English verb 'will' to form the future tense. This requires another verb in German: **werden**. 'I will go to Germany' would be **Ich *werde* nach Deutschland fahren**.

Mögen/möchten 'to like (to), would like (to)'

The modal **mögen** means 'to like (to)' and is often used with reference to people, food or places and activities:

Ich *mag* Emma Watson.	I like Emma Watson.
Er *mag* Tofu.	He likes tofu.
Sie *mögen* Island.	They like Island.
Sie *mag* Tennis.	She likes tennis.

Note that **mögen** can only be used in connection with nouns: **Sie mag *Tennis.*** 'She likes *tennis.*' (=the sport). If you wanted to use a verb, for instance to say 'She likes *playing* tennis', you'll need to use **gern**: **Sie spielt *gern* Tennis.**

The present tense forms of **mögen** are:

ich mag	**wir mögen**
du magst	**ihr mögt**
Sie mögen	**Sie mögen**
er/sie/es mag	**sie mögen**

But **mögen** is most often used in its subjunctive form, **möchten**, which means 'would like to':

Er *möchte* arbeiten.	He would like to work
Er *möchte* ein neues Tablet kaufen.	He would like to buy a new tablet.

The verb endings of **möchten** are regular, except for **er/sie/es**, where there is no **-t** ending:

ich möchte	**wir möchten**
du möchtest	**ihr möchtet**
Sie möchten	**Sie möchten**
er/sie/es möchte	**sie möchten**

Note that **möchten** is sometimes used without a second verb:

Ich möchte einen Kaffee, bitte.	I would like a coffee, please.

Modal verbs used with another verb

As in English, modals are normally used together with another verb.

Er *kann* sehr gut *kochen.*	He can cook very well.
Ich *will* nach New York *fliegen.*	I want to fly to New York.

As you can see there is one main difference between English and German. While in English, the modal verb and the main verb stay together, in German, they are usually separated. The modal verb is the second element of the sentence, and the main verb goes to the end of the sentence:

Ich *kann* morgen nicht *kommen*. — I can't come tomorrow.
Sie *will* eine neue App *kaufen*. — She wants to buy a new app.

Note that the modal verb takes the relevant verb endings, while the main verb is in the infinitive. The infinitive is also *not* prefaced by **zu** 'to' as in English.

Modal verbs in yes or no questions

In *yes or no questions* the modal verb moves – for once – into first position. The second verb remains at the end:

***Kannst* du mir *helfen*?** — Can you help me?
***Darf* ich Sie etwas *fragen*?** — May I ask you something?

Modal and separable verbs

When you use a modal with a separable verb, the separable verb doesn't split apart and goes to the end of the sentence:

Ich *möchte* heute Abend *ausgehen*. — I would like to go out this evening.
Er *muss* die Fotos *ausdrucken*. — He has to print out the photos.

Overview

Here is an overview of modal verb forms. Remember, there are certain patterns:

- All modals except for **sollen** have a vowel change in the **ich**, **du** and **er/sie/es** forms.
- The **ich** and **er/sie/es** forms also drop their endings (no **-e** or **-t**) and are identical.

Note that the irregular forms are all italicised. To check the forms for **möchten**, see above.

	dürfen	*können*	*müssen*	*sollen*	*wollen*	*mögen*
ich	***darf***	***kann***	***muss***	***soll***	***will***	***mag***
du	***darfst***	***kannst***	***musst***	***sollst***	***willst***	***magst***

	dürfen	*können*	*müssen*	*sollen*	*wollen*	*mögen*
Sie	**dürfen**	**können**	**müssen**	**sollen**	**wollen**	**mögen**
er/sie/es	***darf***	***kann***	***muss***	***soll***	***will***	***mag***
wir	**dürfen**	**können**	**müssen**	**sollen**	**wollen**	**mögen**
ihr	**dürft**	**könnt**	**müsst**	**sollt**	**wollt**	**mögt**
Sie	**dürfen**	**können**	**müssen**	**sollen**	**wollen**	**mögen**
sie	**dürfen**	**können**	**müssen**	**sollen**	**wollen**	**mögen**

Did you know?

Although most modal verbs usually appear with another verb in a German sentence, the modal can also appear on its own. This usually occurs in idiomatic expressions or when the context makes it clear:

Können Sie Deutsch?	Can you speak German?
Ich muss jetzt nach Hause.	I have to go home now.
Was soll das?	What's this supposed to mean?

- For modal verbs in the past see Units 22 and 23.
- For the position of modal verbs in subordinate clauses see Unit 28.
- For more information on word order see Unit 29.

Exercise 21.1

Write out all present tense forms (**ich**, **du**, **Sie**, **er/sie/es**, **wir**, **ihr**, **Sie**, **sie**) of (1) **dürfen**; (2) **können**; (3) **müssen**; (4) **sollen**; (5) **wollen**; (6) **mögen**.

Exercise 21.2

Supply the right verb forms of **können**.

Example: ____ Sie Englisch sprechen?
→ ***Können*** Sie Englisch sprechen?

1 Ich ____ gut Ski fahren.
2 ____ du mir eine SMS schicken?
3 Er ____ am Freitag nicht arbeiten.
4 ____ ihr bitte ein bisschen leise sein?
5 Wir ____ uns nächstes Wochenende treffen.
6 Marion ____ sehr gut kochen.

Exercise 21.3

Fill in the correct verb form of the modal verb shown in brackets.

Example: Lena sagt, sie ____ gesünder leben. (wollen)
→ Lena sagt, sie ***will*** gesünder leben.

1 ____ ich Sie etwas fragen? (dürfen)
2 Hier ____ man nicht parken. (dürfen)
3 Kinder ____ die Baustelle nicht betreten. (dürfen)
4 Mein Arzt sagt, ich ____ mehr joggen. (sollen)
5 ____ du immer so spät nach Hause kommen? (müssen)
6 Ich ____ noch einen Tee, bitte. (möchten)
7 Er ____ mit dem Fahrrad fahren. (wollen)
8 ____ ihr uns nicht mal besuchen? (wollen)
9 ____ man hier gut essen gehen? (können)
10 Ich ____ am Wochenende einen Ausflug machen. (wollen)
11 ____ ihr ein Eis essen? (möchten)
12 Er ____ ein neues Smartphone kaufen. (sollen)
13 ____ Sie mir helfen? (können)
14 Du ____ nicht so viel Zeit vor dem Bildschirm verbringen. (sollen)
15 Hier ____ Sie langsam fahren. (müssen)
16 ____ du das bitte wiederholen? (können)

Exercise 21.4

Translate the following sentences. Use both the **du** and **Sie** forms for 'you'.

1 I can cook well.
2 He wants to live healthier.
3 She is supposed to do more sport.
4 We would like to pay.
5 I like Berlin.
6 I would like a coffee, please.
7 Can you help me?
8 May I ask you something?
9 I must go shopping.
10 You mustn't park here.

Checklist

1 What grammatical features do modal verbs have in common?
2 Where is the second verb placed in a sentence with a modal verb?
3 What happens when you use a separable verb, such as **einkaufen** or **ausdrucken**, with a modal?
4 When do you use **mögen**, and when do you use **gern**?
5 How would you translate 'He must not'?

UNIT 22

The present perfect tense

Past tenses in English and German

English and German both have two main tenses for referring to past events, the *present perfect tense* and the *simple past tense*:

Present perfect:	I have talked to him.	**Ich habe mit ihm gesprochen.**
Simple past:	I talked to him.	**Ich sprach mit ihm.**

Different usages

In English, you use the present perfect if a past event is still fairly closely connected to the present and with certain words such as 'just': 'I have just talked to him'. For most other situations you use the simple past: 'I talked to him two years ago'.

In German, the present perfect tense is mostly used for the *spoken* language and the simple past for *written* German. However, in contemporary usage the present perfect can also be increasingly found in writing, usually in less formal contexts. Note that the present perfect tense also refers to events that happened some time ago:

Gestern *hat* es *geregnet.*	It rained yesterday.
Vor zehn Jahren *habe* ich Design *studiert.*	Ten years ago I studied design.

Regular and irregular verbs – an overview

For most verbs in German you form the present perfect tense with a form of **haben** 'to have' + the **past participle** of the main verb: **haben** + **gehört** 'have listened'; **haben** + **getrunken** 'have drunk'.

As in English, some past participles are regular ('listened'/**gehört**), and some are irregular ('drunk'/**getrunken**).

There are also a number of verbs in German which form the present perfect tense with **sein** instead of **haben** + past participle:

Ich *bin* nach Berlin *gefahren.*	I went to Berlin.

Regular verbs in more detail

Formation

The present perfect tense of regular verbs (often called weak verbs) is constructed by using the present tense of **haben** + past participle.

You form the participle by using the stem of the verb (infinitive minus **-en**) and adding **ge-** in front and **-t** at the end:

infinitive		**past participle**
stem + en		**ge** + stem + **t**
kauf-en	→	**ge-kauf-t**
spiel-en		**ge-spiel-t**
sag-en		**ge-sag-t**

Haben *is the finite verb*

When you use this structure, the verb form of **haben** must agree with the subject in the sentence. However, the past participle always stays the same. Look at the complete present perfect tense forms of **spielen** 'to play':

ich habe gespielt	**wir haben gespielt**
du hast gespielt	**ihr habt gespielt**
Sie haben gespielt	**Sie haben gespielt**
er/sie/es hat gespielt	**sie haben gespielt**

Word order

You probably noticed from the examples that **haben** is the second element in a sentence, while the past participle goes to the end of the sentence:

Ich *habe* einen neuen Sweater *gekauft.*	I (have) bought a new sweater.
Gestern *hat* sie Fußball *gespielt.*	Yesterday she played football.

Irregular verbs in more detail

Formation

Irregular verbs (also called strong verbs) form their past participle in most cases by adding **ge-** to the front of the stem and **-en** at the end:

infinitive		*past participle*
stem + en		**ge** + stem + **en**
les-en	→	**ge-les-en**

infinitive		*past participle*
schlaf-en		**ge-schlaf-en**
seh-en		**ge-seh-en**

The majority of irregular verbs also have a *stem vowel* change in their past participle:

infinitive		*past participle*
stem + en		**ge** + stem + **en**
find-en	→	**ge-fund-en**
helf-en		**ge-holf-en**
schreib-en		**ge-schrieb-en**
trink-en		**ge-trunk-en**
nehm-en		**ge-nomm-en**

Word order

As with regular verbs, the past participle goes to the end of the sentence:

Er *hat* ein Bad *genommen.*	Have you seen my mobile?
Wir *haben* eine neue Wohnung *gefunden.*	We (have) found a new flat.
Maik *hat* mir *geholfen.*	Maik (has) helped me.
Sie *haben* viel *getrunken.*	They drank a lot.
***Hast* du mein Handy *gesehen*?**	He had a bath.

Mixed verbs

There is also a group of verbs, often called mixed verbs, which have a stem vowel change like irregular verbs but add the regular **-t** ending. The most important ones are:

infinitive		*past participle*
stem + en		**ge** + stem + **t**
bring-en	→	**ge-brach-t**
denk-en		**ge-dach-t**
wiss-en		**ge-wuss-t**

Examples:

Das *habe* ich mir *gedacht.*	I thought so.
Das *habe* ich nicht *gewusst.*	I didn't know that.

The present perfect tense with *sein*

Verbs of motion take ***sein***

There are two main groups of verbs which form their present perfect tense with a form of **sein** + past participle: verbs of motion indicating movement to or from a place, or those verbs expressing a change of state:

fahren	to go, to drive	→	**Ich *bin* nach München *gefahren*.**
fliegen	to fly		***Bist* du mit Easyjet *geflogen*?**
gehen	to go, to walk		**Er *ist* zu Fuß *gegangen*.**
kommen	to come		**Er *ist* zu spät *gekommen*.**
schwimmen	to swim		**Sie *ist* zwei Kilometer *geschwommen*.**
wachsen	to grow		**Du *bist* aber *gewachsen*!**
reisen	to travel		**Wir *sind* früher viel *gereist*.**
joggen	to jog		**Er *ist* im Park *gejoggt*.**

As you can see, most participles used with **sein** are irregular – they end in **-en** – but there are exceptions such as **gereist** and **gejoggt**.

With regards to word order, the relevant form of **sein** is in second position while the past participle is placed at the end.

More verbs with ***sein***

The following verbs also form the present perfect tense with **sein** and are irregular:

infinitive		*past participle*	
bleiben	→	**geblieben**	to stay
sterben		**gestorben**	to die
werden		**geworden**	to become

Examples:

Wie lange *seid* ihr in den USA *geblieben*?	How long did you stay in the United States?
Sie *ist* Künstlerin *geworden*.	She's become (She became) an artist.

The present perfect tense of *haben* and *sein*

As you can see, **haben** and **sein** play an important role as auxiliary verbs in the formation of the present perfect tense. But it is also important to know their past participle forms.

The past participle of **haben** is **gehabt**:

Er *hat* keine Zeit *gehabt.* — He didn't have any time.

Sein has an irregular past participle – **gewesen**:

Wo *bist* du *gewesen*? — Where have you been?

In spoken German, it is quite common to use the simple past of **haben** and **sein** as an alternative to the present perfect tense. For more details see Unit 23.

Points to watch out for

Verbs with stem endings in ***-d*** *or* ***-t***

Verbs whose stems end in **-d** or **-t** need an extra **e** to form the past participle:

Hast du wieder so viel gered*et*?	Have you been talking so much again?
Der Kaffee hat drei Euro gekost*et*.	The coffee cost three euros.

Verbs with an inseparable prefix

Verbs with an inseparable prefix such as **be-**, **er-**, **ver-** and **zer-** do not put **ge-** in front of the past participle. This applies to regular verbs such as **bezahlen** and **verkaufen** and also to irregular verbs such as **verlieren**:

Er hat das Essen *bezahlt.*	He's paid for the meal.
Wir haben das Auto *verkauft.*	We've sold the car.
Ich habe meinen Terminkalender *verloren.*	I've lost my diary.

Verbs ending in ***-ieren***

Verbs ending in **-ieren** (for example **studieren** and **passieren**) also do not add **ge-** at the front of the past participle:

Er hat in Berlin *studiert.*	He (has) studied in Berlin.
Was ist *passiert*?	What (has) happened?

Separable verbs

Separable verbs form the past participle like other regular or irregular verbs, but *the prefix stays at the front*:

regular	*irregular*
prefix + **ge** + stem + **t**	prefix + **ge** + stem + **en**
aufmach-en → auf-ge-mach-t	**aufsteh-en → auf-ge-stand-en**
einkauf-en → ein-ge-kauf-t	**fernseh-en → fern-ge-seh-en**

Here are some examples:

Hast du den Brief *aufgemacht*?	Have you opened the letter?
Sie haben online *eingekauft*.	They did their shopping online.
Wann bist du *aufgestanden*?	When did you get up?
Ich habe am Abend *ferngesehen*.	I watched TV in the evening.

Working with verb lists

Most German dictionaries, language courses and grammar books have a list of irregular verbs with their past participle forms. We recommend that you look at these lists regularly and learn the most frequently used verbs by heart. As with most other grammar points – the more you practise, the more progress you will make with your language learning.

Did you know?

Verbs which have recently been loaned or adapted from English, such as **posten** 'to post' (online), **twittern** 'to tweet' or **lunchen** 'to have lunch' usually form their present perfect tense with **haben** + regular past participle. An exception is **joggen** 'to jog', which takes **sein**:

Sie hat ein Selfie gepostet.	She posted a selfie.
Hast du gestern noch getwittert?	Did you tweet yesterday?
Ich bin 5 km gejoggt.	I jogged for 5 km.

- For more information on separable verbs see Unit 5.
- For more information on the simple past tense, and when to use it in German, see Unit 23.

Exercise 22.1

Which of these commonly used verbs have an irregular past participle? Place a tick next to them. Mark the ones which take **sein** with an asterisk. One example has been done. Use a verb list if you are not sure about your answers.

arbeiten		hören		nehmen		sprechen	
bleiben	✓*	kaufen		schreiben		stehen	
essen		kommen		schwimmen		treffen	
fahren		lesen		sehen		trinken	
gehen		machen		spielen		wohnen	

Exercise 22.2

Complete the sentences with the correct present perfect form.

Example: Peter ____ seine Schwester ____. (besuchen)
→ Peter ***hat*** seine Schwester ***besucht***.

1 Er ____ bis zwanzig Uhr ____. (arbeiten)
2 Ich ____ gestern ein Konzert ____. (hören)
3 Paula ____ eine neue Jacke ____. (kaufen)
4 Was ____ Sie ____? (sagen)
5 Wir ____ lange auf den Bus ____. (warten)
6 Was ____ du am Wochenende ____? (machen)
7 Ina ____ etwas Neues ____. (posten)
8 Er ____ sehr viel ____. (einkaufen)
9 Ich ____ das Fenster ____. (zumachen)
10 Nada und David ____ beide in Heidelberg ____. (studieren)
11 Er ____ mit seiner Karte ____. (bezahlen)
12 ____ du deine SMS ____? (checken)

Exercise 22.3

Put the following sentences into the present perfect tense. Note that all verbs are irregular.

Example: Ich stehe um acht Uhr auf.
→ Ich ***bin*** um acht Uhr ***aufgestanden***.

1 Ich esse ein Croissant mit Marmelade.
2 Ich trinke Jasmintee.
3 Ich lese die Zeitung.
4 Ich fahre mit dem Fahrrad zur Arbeit.
5 Ich schreibe E-Mails.
6 Ich spreche mit Kunden.
7 Um halb sieben jogge ich.

8 Um acht Uhr treffe ich einen Freund.
9 Wir gehen in ein Restaurant.
10 Um elf Uhr bin ich zu Hause.
11 Ich sehe einen Clip auf YouTube.
12 Ich gehe um Mitternacht ins Bett.
13 Ich schlafe gleich.

Exercise 22.4

Put the following sentences into the present perfect tense. Use the **du**, **Sie** and **ihr** forms for 'you'.

1 Maya worked until nine o'clock.
2 He bought a T-shirt.
3 Martina studied in Berlin.
4 They paid online.
5 He went to a restaurant.
6 They watched television.
7 When did you get up?
8 What did you do yesterday?
9 What has happened?
10 He posted a photo.

Checklist

1 When do you normally use the present perfect tense in German?
2 How do you form the present perfect tense for most verbs?
3 Can you name at least six verbs which use **sein** for the present perfect?
4 How do you form the past participle for regular and irregular verbs?
5 Where does the past participle usually go in a sentence?

UNIT 23

The simple past tense

Usage

The simple past tense is one of the two main tenses used in German to describe past events. Whereas the *present perfect tense* is mostly used for the spoken language and in fairly informal writing, the *simple past* is mainly used in more formal written German. It is often referred to as the *preterite* (**Präteritum**) or the *imperfect* (**Imperfekt**).

Regular and irregular verbs

In English, verbs in the simple past tense are either regular or irregular:

- Regular verbs simply add '-ed' to the verb from the infinitive ('play' → 'play*ed*').
- Irregular verbs usually have a vowel change ('see' → 'saw').

German has a similar pattern:

- Most regular verbs add the required endings to the stem (**spielen** → **ich spiel*te***).
- Many irregular verbs change their stem vowel (**sehen** → **ich s*a*h**). Irregular verbs also have slightly different endings.

All forms are explained in the following paragraphs.

Regular verbs in detail

Formation

To form the simple past tense of regular verbs, take the *stem* and add the appropriate endings:

		mach-en	*spiel-en*	*kauf-en*
ich	**-te**	**mach*te***	**spiel*te***	**kauf*te***
du	**-test**	**mach*test***	**spiel*test***	**kauf*test***
Sie	**-ten**	**mach*ten***	**spiel*ten***	**kauf*ten***
er/sie/es	**-te**	**mach*te***	**spiel*te***	**kauf*te***
wir	**-ten**	**mach*ten***	**spiel*ten***	**kauf*ten***
ihr	**-tet**	**mach*tet***	**spiel*tet***	**kauf*tet***
Sie	**-ten**	**mach*ten***	**spiel*ten***	**kauf*ten***
sie	**-ten**	**mach*ten***	**spiel*ten***	**kauf*ten***

Examples:

Gestern *kaufte* ich eine neue App.	Yesterday I bought a new app.
Am Samstag *spielten* sie Fußball.	On Saturday they played football.
Als Kind *wohnte* er in Berlin.	As a child he lived in Berlin.

Irregular verbs in detail

Similarly to English, many German irregular verbs create their simple past forms by changing the stem vowel. The verb endings in the simple past tense are similar to those in the present tense, except for **ich** and **er/sie/es**, where there is no ending:

		seh-en	*schreib-en*	*geh-en*
ich	–	**sah**	**schrieb**	**ging**
du	**-st**	**sah*st***	**schrieb*st***	**ging*st***
Sie	**-en**	**sah*en***	**schrieb*en***	**ging*en***
er/sie/es	–	**sah**	**schrieb**	**ging**
wir	**-en**	**sah*en***	**schrieb*en***	**ging*en***
ihr	**-t**	**sah*t***	**schrieb*t***	**ging*t***
Sie	**-en**	**sah*en***	**schrieb*en***	**ging*en***
sie	**-en**	**sah*en***	**schrieb*en***	**ging*en***

Examples:

Gestern *sah* ich einen Film.	Yesterday I watched a movie.
Er *schrieb* eine SMS.	He wrote a text message.
Sie *gingen* ins Café.	They went to a cafe.

Mixed verbs

There is also a small number of verbs which change their stem vowel but end in **-te** like the regular verbs. They are often referred to as mixed verbs. The most important ones are:

bringen	→	**brachte**	to bring
denken		**dachte**	to think
kennen		**kannte**	to know (to be acquainted with)
wissen		**wusste**	to know (a fact)

Examples:

Sie d*a*ch*te* an ihre Ferien.	She thought about her holidays.
Das w*u*ss*te* ich nicht.	I didn't know that.

Points to watch out for

Spelling variations

Verbs whose stems end in **-t**, **-n** or **-d** need an extra **e** to make them easier to pronounce:

antwort-en → Er antwort*e*te nicht.	He didn't answer.
regn-en → Gestern regn*e*te es.	Yesterday it rained.
red-en → Sie red*e*ten eine Stunde lang.	They talked for one hour.

Separable verbs

When a separable verb is used in the simple past tense, the prefix is usually separated from the main part of the verb and goes to the end of the sentence:

aufstehen → Ich stand um sechs Uhr auf.	I got up at six o'clock.
hochladen → Er lud die Fotos hoch.	He uploaded the photos.

Haben, *sein* and the modal verbs

Although the simple past tense is mostly used in written German, it can also occur in the spoken language. This particularly applies to **haben** and **sein** and the *modal verbs*. Here they are in more detail.

Haben and sein

Both verbs are somewhat irregular in the simple past tense:

	haben	*sein*
ich	**hatte**	**war**
du	**hattest**	**warst**
Sie	**hatten**	**waren**
er/sie/es	**hatte**	**war**
wir	**hatten**	**waren**
ihr	**hattet**	**wart**
Sie	**hatten**	**waren**
sie	**hatten**	**waren**

Here are some examples:

Ich *hatte* keine Zeit.	I didn't have any time.
Er *hatte* schrecklichen Hunger.	He was terribly hungry.
Er *war* letztes Jahr in London.	He was in London last year.
Wo *wart* ihr denn?	Where were you?

Modal verbs in the simple past tense

Modal verbs behave similarly to 'mixed' verbs. They take the regular **-te** endings, and most of them have a stem vowel change (**ü** → **u**, **ö** → **o**). Here is an overview:

	dürfen	*können*	*müssen*	*sollen*	*wollen*	*mögen*
ich	**durfte**	**konnte**	**musste**	**sollte**	**wollte**	**mochte**
du	**durftest**	**konntest**	**musstest**	**solltest**	**wolltest**	**mochtest**
Sie	**durften**	**konnten**	**mussten**	**sollten**	**wollten**	**mochten**
er/sie/es	**durfte**	**konnte**	**musste**	**sollte**	**wollte**	**mochte**
wir	**durften**	**konnten**	**mussten**	**sollten**	**wollten**	**mochten**
ihr	**durftet**	**konntet**	**musstet**	**solltet**	**wolltet**	**mochtet**
Sie	**durften**	**konnten**	**mussten**	**sollten**	**wollten**	**mochten**
sie	**durften**	**konnten**	**mussten**	**sollten**	**wollten**	**mochten**

Examples:

Er *konnte nicht* kommen.	He couldn't make it.
Wir *mussten* arbeiten.	We had to work.
Ich *wollte* ihr *mailen.*	I wanted to email her.

Learning tip

As a beginner, you will probably use the simple past tense mainly as a 'receptive' skill – when reading texts in German where you mainly have to recognise the words. Often, you may be able to work out the meaning. If you want to learn the forms more systematically, use a list of irregular verbs you'll find in good course books, online, and also at the end of this book.

Did you know?

German fairy tales are written in the simple past, and reading them is an ideal way to familiarise yourself with this tense. You can google many of them, using the key words '**Märchen**' (or 'maerchen') and '**Grimm**'. Alternatively, you can try and find a simplified version for children or parallel texts. In the next exercise you can put this suggestion into practice with a shortened version of the fairy tale *Schneewittchen* (*Snow White*).

Exercise 23.1

Here is an adapted excerpt from the well-known German fairy tale *Schneewittchen* (*Snow White*). Read the text and underline all verbs in the simple past tense. If you can't work out the meaning of a verb, use a verb list or an online dictionary. The first two have been done.

> Nun **war** das arme Kind in dem großen Wald ganz allein. Da **hatte** es große Angst. Es wusste nicht, wo es war und fing an zu laufen, bis es bald Abend wurde. Da sah es ein kleines Häuschen und ging hinein. In dem Haus war alles klein: Da stand ein Tisch mit sieben kleinen Tellern. Außerdem gab es sieben Messer und Gabeln und sieben Becher. An der Wand standen sieben Betten. Schneewittchen, weil es so hungrig und durstig war, aß von jedem Teller ein wenig Gemüse und Brot und trank aus jedem Becher einen Tropfen Wein. Dann, weil es so müde war, legte es sich in ein Bett, aber keins passte; das eine war zu lang, das andere zu kurz, bis endlich das siebente recht war - und darin blieb es liegen, dachte an den lieben Gott und schlief ein.

Decide whether the underlined verbs are regular, irregular or mixed and classify them in the columns below. Can you also work out what the infinitive of each verb is?

regular verbs	*irregular verbs*	*mixed verbs*
	war → sein **hatte → haben**	

Exercise 23.2

Write out the full simple past tense (for all persons: **ich**, **du**, **Sie**, **er/sie/es**, **wir**, **ihr**, **Sie**, **sie**) of the following verbs: (1) **spielen**; (2) **kaufen**; (3) **wohnen**.

Exercise 23.3

Supply the correct endings. In some cases *no ending* is needed.

Example: Er trank__ eine Flasche Bier. → Er ***trank*** eine Flasche Bier.

1 Ich blieb__ eine Woche in Prag.
2 Sah__ du das Fußballspiel im Fernsehen?
3 Luke und Sybille ging__ gestern in den Wellnessclub.
4 Nach dem Essen trank__ wir noch Kaffee.
5 Frau Schneider fuhr__ das erste Mal nach Schottland.
6 Er schrieb__ eine SMS an seine Freundin.
7 Das wusst__ ich nicht.
8 Da bracht__ der Kellner noch einen Nachtisch.

Exercise 23.4

Translate the following sentences.

1 Yesterday I played tennis.
2 I bought a cup of coffee.
3 As a child I lived in Frankfurt.
4 I went to the cinema.
5 We stayed for one week.
6 It was last year.
7 I got up at eight o'clock.
8 I wanted to come, but I didn't have time.

Checklist

1 When do you use the simple past tense?
2 How do you form the simple past tense for regular verbs?
3 What happens to many irregular verbs?
4 Can you name the endings for irregular verbs in the simple past?
5 There are some verbs in the simple past that are often used in *spoken German*. Which ones are they?

UNIT 24

The future tense

Future tenses in English

English has several ways of expressing the future. You can use a structure with 'going to' + verb to refer to something that is going to happen, or you can use 'will' + verb. When the context makes the reference to the future clear, you can also use the continuous present tense form: 'This afternoon I am working from home.'

The two main forms in German

German also has different ways of referring to future events.

- The most common one is to use the *present tense*:

Heute Abend *bleibe* ich zu Hause.	**This evening I am staying at home.**

- Another option is to use **werden** + infinitive:

Am Wochenende *werde* ich auf eine Party *gehen*.	At the weekend I'll go to a party.

Here are both forms in more detail.

Using the present tense

Speakers of German tend to use the *present tense* to refer to the future as long as the context is understood. Look at the following examples:

Wir gehen morgen ins Theater.	We are going to the theatre tomorrow.
Fahrt ihr in den Ferien nach Italien?	Will you be going to Italy in the holidays?
Ich mache später einen Salat.	I'll be making a salad later.

As you have probably noticed, normally an expression of time (**morgen** 'tomorrow', **in den Ferien** 'in the holidays', **später** 'later') is used, which makes the reference to the future quite clear.

Expressions indicating the future

There are a number of words and expressions in German which give indications of a time in the future. They include:

bald	soon
später	later
morgen	tomorrow
übermorgen	the day after tomorrow
nachher	after(wards)
in zehn Minuten	in ten minutes
heute Abend	this evening
in einer Woche	in a week's time
in zwei Wochen	in two weeks' time
nächsten Monat	next month
in einem Jahr	in a year's time

Whenever you are using expressions such as these, you can quite easily use the present tense to talk about the future as the context will be evident. Look at the following examples:

Ich bin bald fertig.	I'll be ready soon.
Wir kommen später.	We'll come later.
Er hat morgen eine Prüfung.	He's got an exam tomorrow.
Sie können es in 10 Minuten abholen.	You can collect it in 10 minutes.
In einer Woche sind wir in Spanien.	In a week's time we'll be in Spain.
Habt ihr nächsten Monat Zeit?	Will you be free next month?

Expressions of time as the first element

It is not uncommon to start a sentence with an expression of time in German. If this happens make sure that the verb remains the second element and that the subject follows the verb:

time expression	*verb*	*subject*	*other elements*
Morgen	**bleibe**	**ich**	**zu Hause.**
In einer Woche	**sind**	**wir**	**in Spanien.**

Using *werden* + infinitive

The other way of referring to the future in German is using **werden** + infinitive:

Ich werde dich anrufen.	I will call you.
Wirst du zu Hause sein?	Will you be at home?
Er wird nächste Saison für Dortmund spielen.	He will be playing for Dortmund next season.
Das Update wird in zwei Wochen kommen.	The update will be available in two weeks' time.
Sie werden im August umziehen.	They will move house in August.

As you have probably noticed, this structure is quite similar to the English future tense, formed with 'will' + the infinitive of the main verb.

Points to watch out for

Werden is an irregular verb

Be aware that **werden** is an irregular verb. Here are all the forms:

ich werde	**wir werden**
du w*irst*	**ihr werdet**
Sie werden	**Sie werden**
er/sie/es w*ird*	**sie werden**

Note the following irregularities:

- **werden** has a stem vowel change **e** → **i** with **du** and **er/sie/es**: **du wirst**, **er/sie/es wird**.
- The form for **du** also drops the **d** from the stem: **du wirst**.
- There is no additional ending with **er/sie/es**: **er wird**.

Word order

In the future tense, **werden** is the second element in a sentence, and its verb form needs to agree with the subject. The second verb is always in the infinitive and is placed at the end of the sentence:

Sie *werden* im August *umziehen*.
Das Update *wird* in zwei Wochen *kommen*.

Remember that if you start the sentence with an expression of time, the subject will move directly behind the appropriate form of **werden**.

Usage

To express the future, Germans normally use the present tense. The future tense with **werden** + infinitive tends to be used when emphasising a point or indicating probability, often used in connection with **wohl** probably:

Sie wird im Juni heiraten.	She will get married in June.
Morgen wird es wohl regnen.	Tomorrow it will probably rain.
Er wird wohl heute Abend ankommen.	He'll probably arrive this evening.

Tips for English speakers

As with all other tenses, German does not have a progressive form of the future tense ('I will be working'). Only the 'standard' future tense is used in German: **Ich werde arbeiten**.

Also avoid using the modal verb **wollen** + infinitive to talk about the future. **Ich will arbeiten** does *not* mean 'I will work'. It means 'I want to work'.

Did you know?

The verb **werden** is quite versatile and can take on various roles in German. When it stands on its own it normally means 'to become':

Sie *wird* Architektin. She'll become an architect.

In more advanced structures it can mean 'would', and also form the passive:

Ich *würde* freundlicher sein.	I would be more friendly.
Die Autos *werden* in China produziert.	The cars are produced in China.

Exercise 24.1

Write out the full present tense for **werden** for all persons: **ich**, **du**, **Sie**, **er/sie/es**, **wir**, **ihr**, **Sie**, **sie**.

Exercise 24.2

Underline the words and expressions which indicate the future.

Example: Am Dienstag gehen wir ins Restaurant.
→ <u>Am Dienstag</u> gehen wir ins Restaurant.

1 Morgen fahre ich zu meinen Eltern.
2 Bitte rufen Sie in einer halben Stunde wieder an.
3 Nächsten Monat habe ich wieder mehr Zeit.
4 Das Fußballspiel findet am Freitag statt.
5 Wir wollen heute ins Fitnesscenter gehen.
6 Sehen wir uns später?
7 Habt ihr bald Zeit?
8 Wohin fahrt ihr in den Sommerferien?

Exercise 24.3

Make complete sentences using the future tense with **werden** and say what these people will do at the weekend.

Example: ich / einkaufen gehen
→ Ich ***werde*** am Wochenende einkaufen gehen.

1 Freya / ein Buch über Yoga lesen
2 Jan / eine Radtour machen
3 Louis und Anna / zu Hause bleiben
4 ich / Freunde besuchen
5 die Nachbarn / einen Computerspielabend machen
6 Valentin / an seinem Blog schreiben
7 Annett / im Supermarkt jobben
8 wir / auf eine Party gehen

Exercise 24.4

Translate the following sentences. Use (*a*) the present tense and then (*b*) the future tense with **werden**. Use the **du**, **Sie** and **ihr** forms for 'you'.

1 I'll work on Friday.
2 I'll come later.
3 He'll go to the cinema tomorrow.
4 At the weekend we'll stay at home.
5 Tomorrow it will rain.
6 What are you doing later?
7 What are you doing in the summer holidays?

Checklist

1 When can you use the present tense to refer to future events in German?
2 How do you form the future tense?
3 What irregularities are there in the different forms of the verb **werden**?
4 What position does the second verb have in a future tense sentence?

UNIT 25

Prepositions

What are prepositions?

Prepositions are frequently used words such as 'from', 'on', 'with' and 'under' which define the relation between different items in a sentence. They can give information about:

- direction: 'I'm *from* Germany',
- position: 'The book is *on* the table', or
- time: 'She will come *at* eight o'clock'.

Using prepositions in German

The function of prepositions in English and German is very similar. What complicates matters in German is that prepositions usually require a certain case. It does not matter in a sentence such as **Ich bin *aus* Deutschland** 'I'm *from* Germany' because there is no article. But for any other structures where the preposition, for instance, precedes an article or possessive, you must be aware of the case the preposition takes and the changes this may imply.

Prepositions and cases – an overview

In German, prepositions can be divided into different groups according to the case they require. The following sections will look at each of the relevant cases (accusative, dative and genitive), list the various prepositions, give their meanings and explain what specific changes you'll need to make to the words following them.

If you would like to remind yourself of the case system, go to Units 11–15.

Prepositions + accusative case in more detail

The following prepositions are always followed by the accusative case:

bis	until
durch	through

für	for
gegen	against, around
ohne	without
um	around, at

Usage in both languages

The meanings and usage of these prepositions are very similar in English and German. Here are some examples:

Bis **morgen.**	Until tomorrow.
Gehen wir ***durch*** **den Park?**	Shall we go through the park?
Danke ***für*** **das Geschenk.**	Thanks for the present.
Er spielt ***gegen*** **den Sieger.**	He plays against the winner.
Ich reise nie ***ohne*** **meinen E-Reader.**	I never travel without my e-reader.
Ich komme ***um*** **fünf Uhr.**	I'll come at five o'clock.

Note that **gegen** can also refer to time: **gegen acht Uhr** 'around eight o'clock'. **Um** is used for directions – **um die Welt** 'around the world' – and for time: **um fünf Uhr** 'at five o'clock'.

Endings in the accusative case

Remember that in the accusative case, articles, possessives and the negative **kein** referring to masculine nouns take **-en**. Feminine equivalents all end in **-e**. As for neuter forms, there is a **-s** for the definite article, but the other determiners don't require specific endings. Look at the examples:

Ich reise nie ohne mein*en* E-Reader. (*m*)
Was für ein*e* Überraschung. (*f*)
Was für ein Geschenk. (*nt*)

Short forms

Note that in less formal contexts some prepositions and the definite article **das** can be joined together: **durch das → durchs**; **für das → fürs**; **um das → ums**:

Vielen Dank fürs Geschenk.	Many thanks for the present.
Sie geht ums Haus.	She goes around the house.

Prepositions + dative case in more detail

The following prepositions always require the dative case:

aus	from, out of
außer	apart from

bei	at, near
gegenüber	opposite
mit	with, by (for means of transport)
nach	after, to
seit	since, for
von	from
zu	to

Endings in the dative case

Remember that the required endings for the dative case are **-em** for masculine and neuter nouns and **-er** for feminine nouns:

Sie fährt mit d*em* Zug. (*m*)	She goes by train.
Sie fährt mit d*er* U-Bahn. (*f*)	She goes by tube.
Sie fährt mit d*em* Fahrrad. (*nt*)	She goes by bike.

Short forms

Note that in the following instances the prepositions and the definite article are normally joined together: **bei dem → beim**; **von dem → vom**; **zu der → zur**; and **zu dem → zum**.

Ich komme vom Flughafen.	I am coming from the airport.
Er geht zur Apotheke.	He goes to the pharmacy.

Usage in both languages

Although many of the prepositions are similar to English, there are quite a few instances where the usage of the German is different:

- To say where somebody is *from*, you would use **aus** in German:

  Sie kommen *aus* Berlin. — They come from Berlin.

- The preposition **bei** can specify a location and is also used to say that you were seeing, visiting, or staying with another person:

  Potsdam liegt *bei* Berlin. — Potsdam is near Berlin.
  Sie war *beim* Arzt. — She was at the doctor's.

- When referring to means of transport, German uses **mit**:

  Er fährt *mit* dem Auto. — He is travelling by car.

- To say that you go by foot, you'll need **zu**:

  Ich gehe *zu* Fuß. — I walk.

- When asking for directions of places **zu** is used in German, but when referring to towns or most countries you need **nach**:

Wie komme ich *zum* Bahnhof? — How do I get to the railway station?
Ich fahre *nach* New York. — I am going to New York.

For all these contexts, you have to learn the corresponding preposition in German.

Prepositions + accusative or dative in more detail

When to use the accusative and when to use the dative

Some prepositions in German take *either* the accusative *or* the dative case, depending on whether the emphasis is on movement or position. The one you will probably most frequently use at this level is **in**:

Sie geht *ins* (*in das*) Café. – Indicates movement: 'going to/into the cafe'. **In** is followed by the *accusative* case.

Sie war *im* (*in dem*) Café. – The emphasis is on position: 'being in the cafe'. **In** is followed by the *dative* case.

Prepositions using both cases

All these prepositions can take either the accusative or the dative:

an	at, on
auf	on, on top of
hinter	behind
in	in
neben	next to, beside
über	over, above, across
unter	under, among
vor	in front of, before
zwischen	between

Here are some more examples of this group of prepositions in use:

Ich lege das Magazin *auf den* Tisch. (*accusative*)	I put the magazine on the table.
Das Magazin liegt *auf dem* Tisch. (*dative*)	The magazine is on the table.
Er hängt das Poster *an die* Wand. (*accusative*)	He puts the poster on the wall.
Das Poster hängt *an der* Wand. (*dative*)	The poster is on the wall.
Sie legt das I-Pad *aufs* Regal. (*accusative*)	She puts the iPad on the shelf.
Das I-Pad ist *auf dem* Regal. (*dative*)	The iPad is on the shelf.

Short forms

Note that **in das** is often shortened to **ins** and **in dem** to **im**:

Er geht *ins* Kino. Er war *im* Kino.

It is also very common to say **aufs** instead of **auf das**:

Sie legt das I-Pad *aufs* Regal.

Prepositions + genitive case in more detail

There are also a few prepositions which take the genitive case. The most important are:

trotz	despite
während	during
wegen	because of, due to
(an)statt	instead of

You will probably use them more frequently at an advanced level.

***Während* des Sommers lebt er in Italien.**	During the summer he lives in Italy.
***Wegen* ihrer Allergie kann sie keinen Weizen essen.**	Because of her allergy she can't eat wheat.
***Trotz* des schlechten Wetters fuhr er mit dem Fahrrad.**	Despite the bad weather he went by bike.

As you can see the required endings in the genitive case are **-es** for masculine and neuter nouns and **-er** for feminine nouns. Masculine and neuter nouns usually also add **-es** for short nouns and **-s** for longer nouns.

Prepositions and plural forms

For the plural forms in connections with prepositions, see Units 11 and 13-15.

Learning tip

Don't feel overwhelmed by the sheer number of prepositions. As a beginner you will not use all of them. In a good course book they will be introduced in groups so that it is easier for you to memorise them.

Also try to learn them in context, so that you will know when to use them, and make sure that you know which prepositions take which cases.

Summary

Here is a summary:

accusative	dative	accusative or dative	genitive
bis until	**aus** from, out of	**an** at, on	**trotz** despite
durch through	**außer** apart from	**auf** on, on top of	**während** during
für for	**bei** at, near	**hinter** behind	**wegen** because of, due to
gegen against, around	**gegenüber** opposite	**in** in, into	**(an)statt** instead of
		neben next to	
ohne without	**mit** with, by (for means of transport)	**über** over, above, across	
um around, at	**nach** after, to	**unter** under, among	
	seit since, for		
	von from	**vor** in front of, before	
	zu to		
		zwischen between	

Did you know?

Using mnemonics or memory aids can be a useful way to remember vocabulary or certain grammatical features. An example of how you could memorise the German prepositions which are followed by the accusative is: **fudg-o**. This represents the most frequently used accusative prepositions: **f**ür, **u**m, **d**urch, **g**egen, **o**hne.

Exercise 25.1

Supply an appropriate preposition from the list below. The first one has been done.

nach zu mit in für im ins gegen bei an
gegenüber zum zur für um ~~in~~ während ~~aus~~

1 Max Störzl kommt ***aus*** Österreich, aber lebt ***in*** Berlin.
2 Sie wohnt ____ ihrer Tante.
3 Am Wochenende fährt sie ____ Hamburg.
4 Meistens fährt er ____ dem Mountainbike, manchmal geht er ____ Fuß.
5 Gehst du später ____ die Kneipe?
6 Kommst du heute Abend mit ____ Kino?
7 Ich war erst gestern ____ Kino.
8 Das Flachbildschirm hängt ____ der Wand.
9 Treffen wir uns ____ acht Uhr?
10 Wie komme ich ____ Bahnhof?
11 Ist das der Weg ____ Pauluskirche?
12 Die Touristeninformation ist ____ dem Museum.
13 Bayern München hat ____ Real Madrid gewonnen.
14 Ich bin ____ den Vorschlag.
15 ____ der Ferien habe ich gejobbt.

Exercise 25.2

Now go through Exercise 25.1 again. Place the prepositions in the relevant column below:

only accusative	*only dative*	*accusative or dative*	*genitive*
	aus	***in***	

Exercise 25.3

Fill in the correct endings.

Example: Gehst du heute i__ Kino? (*nt*) → Gehst du heute ***ins*** Kino?

1 Er ist gegen d__ Plan. (*m*)
2 Ohne sein__ Spielekonsole kann er nicht mehr leben. (*f*)
3 Gehen wir durch d__ Park? (*m*)
4 Nach d__ Schule will er ein Gapjahr machen. (*f*)
5 Mit d__ Fahrrad bist du aber schneller. (*nt*)
6 Er macht seit ein__ Jahr einen Pilateskurs. (*nt*)
7 Wie weit ist es bis z__ Bahnhof? (*m*)
8 Von d__ Haltestelle sind es nur fünf Minuten bis nach Hause. (*f*)
9 Wir gehen heute i__ Restaurant. (*nt*)
10 Wie ist das Essen i__ neuen Restaurant? (*nt*)
11 Am Wochenende war er bei sein__ Eltern. (*pl*)
12 Fährst du zu dein__ Freunden? (*pl*)

Exercise 25.4

Translate the following sentences. Use the **du** and **Sie** forms for 'you'.

1 We're walking through the park.
2 He is against the plan.
3 I go by car.
4 Marion goes by bike.
5 How do I get to the railway station?
6 We are going to a restaurant.
7 Are you going to the cinema?
8 At the weekend I am going to Berlin.

Checklist

1 Can you remember which prepositions always use the accusative case?
2 Can you name a few prepositions that always require the dative case?
3 There are a number of prepositions which can take either the accusative or the dative case. When do these prepositions require the accusative, when the dative?
4 Can you remember what shortened forms such as **aufs**, **beim** and **im** stand for? Can you name two other examples?

UNIT 26
Adjective endings

What are adjectives?

Adjectives are words that provide more information about a noun: 'The laptop is *new*.' 'The exhibition is *interesting*.' 'It is a *boring* book.'

Usage in English

As you can see from the examples, an adjective can either follow or precede a noun. In English, this causes no problems, as the adjective does not change its form.

Adjective endings in German

In German, on the other hand, the position of the adjective makes a big difference.

Adjectives after nouns

If the adjective comes after the noun it describes, it doesn't change:

Der Laptop ist *neu*.	The laptop is new.
Die Ausstellung ist *interessant*.	The exhibition is interesting.

Adjectives preceding a noun take specific endings

If the adjective is placed before the noun, you add an ending. Look at the following examples:

Der Laptop ist *neu*.	→	**Es ist ein neu*er* Laptop.**
Die Ausstellung ist *interessant*.		**Es ist eine interessant*e* Ausstellung.**
Das Buch ist *langweilig*.		**Es ist ein langweilig*es* Buch.**

Points to consider

As you have probably realised, the required ending of the adjective

- reflects the gender of the noun it precedes.

Also, there are two other points to consider:

- what case the noun has
- whether the adjective is connected to an indefinite article like **ein** or **eine**, to a definite article like **der**, **die** or **das**, or whether it appears before a noun without an article.

This may sound more complicated than it actually is. In practice many endings are identical, and there are certain patterns you can apply.

Adjectives with the indefinite article

Nominative case

You have just seen how the adjective endings work in the nominative case:

Es ist ein neu*er* Laptop.	It is a new laptop.
Es ist ein*e* interessant*e* Ausstellung.	It is an interesting exhibition.
Es ist ein langweilig*es* Buch.	It is a boring book.

Note that in the absence of a definite article (**der**, **die**, **das**), the adjective takes the definite article endings (**-er**, **-e**, **-(e)s**) and 'marks' the noun, i.e. indicates whether it is masculine, feminine or neuter.

Accusative case

The endings in the accusative case are the same as in the nominative, with the exception of adjectives preceding masculine nouns, which add **-en**:

Saskia hat ein*en* neu*en* Laptop.	Saskia has got a new laptop.
Er besucht ein*e* interessant*e* Ausstellung.	He is going to an interesting exhibition.
Er liest ein langweilig*es* Buch.	He is reading a boring book.

Dative case

The adjective endings in the dative case are relatively easy – they all add **-en**. Don't forget to make the necessary changes to the indefinite articles:

Mit ein*em* neu*en* Laptop kann man schneller arbeiten.	With a new laptop one can work faster.
Sie trafen sich auf ein*er* interessant*en* Ausstellung.	They met at an interesting exhibition.
Mit ein*em* langweilig*en* Buch kann er nichts anfangen.	A boring book is of no use to him.

*Possessives and **kein***

Note that all these endings apply also when the adjective follows the *possessives* (**mein**, **dein**, **sein** etc.) and the negative **kein**:

Das ist *mein* neu*er* Laptop.	This is my new laptop.
Das ist *keine* gut*e* Ausstellung.	This is not a good exhibition.

Plural forms

The indefinite article **ein** 'a' cannot refer to the plural. After the *possessives* and **kein**, all adjectives add **-en**. See the table below for more details.

Summary – adjective endings after the indefinite article

Here is an overview of all adjective endings after the indefinite article. The endings for the genitive case have been added, although you will probably use them only at a later stage.

	masculine	*feminine*	*neuter*	*plural*
nominative	**ein neu*er* Laptop**	**eine interessant*e* Ausstellung**	**ein langweilig*es* Buch**	**meine alt*en* DVDs**
accusative	**einen neu*en* Laptop**	**eine interessant*e* Ausstellung**	**ein langweilig*es* Buch**	**meine alt*en* DVDs**
dative	**einem neu*en* Laptop**	**einer interessant*en* Ausstellung**	**einem langweilig*en* Buch**	**meinen alt*en* DVDs**
genitive	**eines neu*en* Laptops**	**einer interessant*en* Ausstellung**	**eines langweilig*en* Buches**	**meiner alt*en* DVDs**

Try to remember that

- the *nominative* and *accusative singular* forms have the endings associated with the definite article
- all *dative*, *genitive* and *plural* endings take **-en**.

Adjectives with no article

Similar pattern to that with the indefinite article

Adjective endings when there is no article are very similar to the ones that appear with the indefinite article. In fact, they are identical in the nominative and accusative singular, where the adjective functions as a 'marker' for the noun.

Nominative case

Here are some examples in the nominative case:

Deutsch*er* Wein ist nicht teuer.	German wine is not expensive.
Italienisch*e* Salami ist sehr populär.	Italian salami is very popular.
Polnisch*es* Bier schmeckt gut.	Polish beer tastes nice.

Accusative case

In the accusative case, adjectives before a masculine noun add **-en**:

Er mag deutsch*en* Wein.	He likes German wine.

The feminine and neuter forms are the same as the nominative:

Sie liebt italienisch*e* Salami.	She loves Italian salami.
Er trinkt viel polnisch*es* Bier.	He drinks a lot of Polish beer.

Dative case

Endings in the dative case are a bit different. In the absence of an article, the adjective takes the typical dative endings (**-em**, **-er**, **-em**):

Fisch passt zu deutsch*em* Wein.	Fish goes well with German wine.
Was hältst du von italienisch*er* Salami?	What do you think of Italian salami?
Von polnisch*em* Bier bekommt man keinen Kater.	You won't get a hangover from Polish beer.

Plural forms

In the plural the nominative and accusative cases add **-e**, and the dative needs the **-en** ending. See the table below for more details.

Summary – adjective endings with no article

Here is a full list of adjective endings when there is no article. The endings of the genitive case have also been added.

	masculine	*feminine*	*neuter*	*plural*
nominative	**deutsch*er* Wein**	**italienisch*e* Salami**	**polnisch*es* Bier**	**deutsch*e* Touristen**
accusative	**deutsch*en* Wein**	**italienisch*e* Salami**	**polnisch*es* Bier**	**deutsch*e* Touristen**
dative	**deutsch*em* Wein**	**italienisch*er* Salami**	**polnisch*em* Bier**	**deutsch*en* Touristen**
genitive	**deutsch*en* Weines**	**italienisch*er* Salami**	**polnisch*en* Bieres**	**deutsch*er* Touristen**

Try to remember that

- in the absence of an article, the adjective takes the ending associated with the relevant definite article.

Adjectives with the definite article

Nominative case

In the nominative case the definite articles (**der**, **die**, **das**) clearly 'mark' the gender of the noun. All adjectives add **-e**:

Der blau*e* Rock sieht cool aus.	The blue skirt looks cool.
Die grün*e* Jacke steht ihr.	The green jacket suits her.
Das blau*e* T-Shirt ist aus London.	The blue T-shirt is from London.

Accusative case

The endings are identical to the ones in the nominative, with the exception of masculine nouns, where **-en** is added:

Heute trägt sie d*en* blau*en* Rock.	She is wearing the blue skirt today.
Sie mag die grün*e* Jacke.	She likes the green jacket.
Er kauft das blau*e* T-Shirt.	He is buying the blue T-shirt.

Dative case

The dative case is relatively straightforward: all adjectives add **-en**:

Sie trägt ihren Mantel mit dem blau*en* Rock/der grün*en* Jacke/dem blau*en* T-Shirt.

Plural forms

As in the dative, all plural forms add **-en**. See the table below for more details.

Dieser 'this'

The determiner **dieser** 'this, these' follows the pattern of the definite article and requires the same adjective endings.

Summary – adjective endings after the definite article

Here is an overview of all adjective endings after the definite article. As before, genitive endings are included.

	masculine	*feminine*	*neuter*	*plural*
nominative	**der blau*e* Rock**	**die grün*e* Jacke**	**das blau*e* Hemd**	**die neu*en* Schuhe**
accusative	**den blau*en* Rock**	**die grün*e* Jacke**	**das blau*e* Hemd**	**die neu*en* Schuhe**
dative	**dem blau*en* Rock**	**der grün*en* Jacke**	**dem blau*en* Hemd**	**den neu*en* Schuhen**
genitive	**des blau*en* Rockes**	**der grün*en* Jacke**	**des blau*en* Hemdes**	**der neu*en* Schuhe**

Try to remember that

- there are only two adjective endings after the definite article, **-e** and **-en**
- **-e** is used for all singular forms in the nominative and accusative case, apart from masculine nouns in the accusative
- **-en** is used for all dative and genitive forms, all plural endings and the masculine accusative forms.

Adjectives in the comparative and superlative

Adjectives in the comparative and superlative – when in front of a noun – change their endings accordingly:

Sie haben ein größer*es* Haus gekauft.	They bought a bigger house.
Dies ist der hipst*e* Club in Berlin.	This is the trendiest club in Berlin.
Er trägt sein best*es* Hemd.	He is wearing his best shirt.
Sie produzieren den best*en* Biowein.	They produce the best organic wine.

Note that there is no **am** before the superlative form when it occurs in front of the noun.

Did you know?

Some adjectives referring to colour in German don't have any endings in standard German when they appear before a noun. They include **lila** 'lilac, purple' and **rosa** 'pink':

Er hat eine lila Handyhülle. He has a purple mobile phone case.
Sie trägt einen rosa Rock. She is wearing a pink skirt.

- For information about the comparative and superlative of adjectives see Unit 20.

Exercise 26.1

Fill in the correct adjective endings and any dative plural endings after the indefinite article or a possessive.

Example: Das ist ein gut__ Tablet. (*nt*) → Das ist ein gut***es*** Tablet.

1 Es ist ein schön__ Tag. (*m*)
2 Das ist ein gut__ Preis. (*m*)
3 Sie hat einen neu__ Laptop gekauft. (*m*)
4 Haben Sie eine neu__ Wohnung? (*f*)
5 Anja telefoniert mit einer gut__ Freundin. (*f*)
6 Ist er wirklich mit seinem alt__ Auto nach Italien gefahren? (*nt*)
7 Zu seinem blau__ Hemd trägt er eine cool__ Sweatjacke. (*nt* / *f*)
8 Sind das seine neu__ Schuhe? (*pl*)
9 Sie hat ihre schönst__ Sachen angezogen. (*pl*)
10 Er trifft sich mit seinen best__ Freunde__. (*pl*)

Exercise 26.2

Supply the correct endings for these commonly used expressions. Note that phrases marked with an asterisk take the accusative case. This affects masculine nouns such as **Abend**. 'Good evening' is therefore **Gut*en* Abend**.

Example: Lieb__ Freunde. → Lieb***e*** Freunde.

1 Lieb__ Susanne.
2 Lieb__ Daniel.
3 Lieb__ Eltern.
4 Gut__ Morgen.* (*m*)
5 Gut__ Tag.* (*m*)
6 Gut__ Nacht.* (*f*)
7 Mit freundlich__ Gruß. (*m*)
8 In groß__ Liebe. (*f*)
9 Mit viel__ Küssen. (*pl*)
10 Mit freundlich__ Grüßen. (*pl*)

Exercise 26.3

Fill in the correct endings.

Example: Der grün__ Rock ist sehr modisch.
→ Der grün*e* Rock ist sehr modisch.

1 Das grün__ Hemd gefällt mir.
2 Die blau__ Jacke ist auch nicht schlecht.
3 Die weiß__ Bluse trage ich am liebsten.
4 Passt sie denn zu der weiß__ Bluse?
5 Der blau__ Anzug war sehr teuer.
6 Ich ziehe den blau__ Anzug fast jeden Tag an.
7 Mit dem blau__ Anzug trage ich am liebsten die rot__ Krawatte.
8 Die italienisch__ Schuhe sehen wirklich trendy aus.

Exercise 26.4

Translate the following sentences.

1 Good morning.
2 Good night.
3 It is a beautiful day.
4 He has bought a new laptop.
5 I like Italian wine.
6 The red jacket is cool.
7 I like the blue suit.
8 I wear the black shoes.

Checklist

1 Adjectives can be placed before and after a noun. Which ones need to take an ending?
2 Can you remember all the adjective endings after an indefinite article?
3 What happens to adjective endings in the absence of an article?
4 After the definite article there are only two endings: **-e** and **-en**. Can you remember which forms take the **-e**?

UNIT 27
Numbers and dates

Numbers and dates in English and German

Numbers and dates are important in all languages. There are many similarities in the way English and German numbers are formed and used, but ordinal numbers in German ('first', 'second' etc.) need endings like any other adjective.

Numbers

Numbers 0–20

These are the cardinal numbers from 0 to 20 in German:

0 **null**	
1 **eins**	11 **elf**
2 **zwei**	12 **zwölf**
3 **drei**	13 **dreizehn**
4 **vier**	14 **vierzehn**
5 **fünf**	15 **fünfzehn**
6 **sechs**	16 **sechzehn**
7 **sieben**	17 **siebzehn**
8 **acht**	18 **achtzehn**
9 **neun**	19 **neunzehn**
10 **zehn**	20 **zwanzig**

Similarly to English, in German **zehn** 'ten' is added to form the numbers 13 to 19. Note that the **s** is dropped in **sechzehn**, and **siebzehn** drops the **en**.

Numbers 20–99

The tens

20 **zwanzig**	60 **sechzig**
30 **dreißig**	70 **siebzig**
40 **vierzig**	80 **achtzig**
50 **fünfzig**	90 **neunzig**

Note that **dreißig** is spelt with **ß** instead of **z**. Again the **s** is dropped in **sechzig** and the **en** in **siebzig**.

Numbers over 20

Numbers over 20 are formed by giving the unit number, then **und** and then the tens. This is different from English, where you first have the tens and then the single number: twenty-one, twenty-two etc. In German, it is (literally translated) one-and-twenty, two-and-twenty etc. Here are more examples:

21 **einundzwanzig**
32 **zweiunddreißig**
44 **vierundvierzig**
56 **sechsundfünfzig** etc.

Eins drops the **s** for numbers above 20 (**einunddreißig**, **einundvierzig** etc.).

Numbers 100 and above

Start with the number of hundreds and then add the tens and units as explained above:

100 **(ein)hundert**
202 **zweihundertzwei**
310 **dreihundertzehn**
456 **vierhundertsechsundfünfzig**
889 **achthundertneunundachtzig**

In contemporary German there is normally no **und** added after **hundert**. This also applies to numbers above 1000:

1020 **(ein)tausendzwanzig**
7455 **siebentausendvierhundertfünfundfünfzig**
450 000 **vierhundertfünfzigtausend**

Other points to watch out for

Special number ***eins***

You have already seen that **eins** drops the **s** when used in numbers above 20: **einundzwanzig**, **einhundert**, **eintausend**.

When it appears on its own in front of a noun it is normally treated as an adjective and takes the same endings as **ein**, the indefinite article: **Er möchte *einen* Kaffee. Er läuft *eine* Meile.**

When used with time, you say: **Es ist ein Uhr** or **Es ist eins.**

Long words

You have probably noticed that all numbers in German are written as one word. Only numbers above a million are separated:

1 100 000 **eine Million einhunderttausend**
10 800 000 **zehn Millionen achthunderttausend**

Dates – ordinal numbers

Formation

Dates in German ('the first', 'the second') end in:

- **-te** with numbers up to 19, and
- **-ste** with numbers from 20 upwards.

These numbers ('first', 'second' etc.) are called *ordinal numbers*. Because ordinal numbers usually provide more information about a noun ('the first of February'), they take the appropriate adjective ending.

This means that if, for instance, an ordinal number is preceded by a preposition taking the dative case, it takes the dative ending, adding **-n**:

am **vierzehn*ten* Mai**	on the fourteenth of May
am **dreißig*sten* April**	on the thirtieth of April

Here are all forms in more detail.

Ordinal numbers from 'first' to 'nineteenth'

For numbers up to and including the nineteenth add **-te**:

ers*te*
zwei*te*
drit*te*
vier*te*
fünf*te*
sechs*te*
sieb*te*
ach*te*
zehn*te*

zwölf*te*
vierzehn*te* etc.

Heute ist der *erste* Januar.	Today is the first of January.
Der *zehnte* August ist ein Samstag.	The tenth of August is a Saturday.

Note the slightly irregular forms: **der *erste*** ('the first'), **der *dritte*** ('the third'), **der *siebte*** ('the seventh') and **der achte** ('the eighth').

From 'twentieth' upwards

For all numbers from 'the twentieth' upwards add **-ste**:

einundzwanzig*ste*
einunddreißig*ste*

Der *einundzwanzigste* Mai passt mir.	The twenty-first of January suits me.
Heute ist der *fünfundzwanzigste* Juni.	Today is the twenty-fifth of June.

Ordinal numbers with dative endings

To indicate on which date something happens, you use **am** in German.

As **am** (**an** + **dem**) is followed by the dative case, an extra **-n** needs to be added to the **-te** and **-ste** endings:

Ich fahre *am ersten* Juli nach Hamburg.	I'm going to Hamburg on the first of July.
***Am fünfzehnten* Mai beginnt mein Urlaub.**	My holidays start on the fifteenth of May.
Habt ihr *am dreißigsten* Zeit?	Are you free on the thirtieth (of this month)?

More expressions

Other frequently used prepositions which require the dative case are **seit** 'since'/'from', **von** 'from' and **bis zu** '(until) to':

Er kennt sie *seit dem* ersten Juni.	He has known her since the first of June.
Das Geschäft ist *vom* dritten *bis zum* zweiundzwanzigsten geschlossen.	The shop is closed from the third to the twenty-second.

Years in German

When referring to years, German does not use the preposition 'in' as in English:

Ich bin 1991 geboren. (= **neunzehnhunderteinundneunzig**)	I was born in 1991.
2014 fand die Fußball-WM in Brasilien statt. (= zweitausendvierzehn)	In 2014 the football world championship took place in Brazil.

It is possible to say **im Jahre**, but this sounds rather old-fashioned:

Ich bin im Jahre 1991 geboren. I was born in the year 1991.

Did you know?

To avoid confusion when dealing with large numbers, German often uses a full stop or a space where there would be a comma in English:

10,000	→	10.000 or 10 000
243,000	→	243.000 or 243 000
1,000,000	→	1.000.000 or 1 000 000

When writing the date in figures, Germans add a full stop after the ordinal number: **14. May**; **am 30. April**.

- For more information on prepositions and cases see Unit 25.
- Adjective endings are explained in Unit 26.

Exercise 27.1

Write out the following numbers.

Example: 435 → vierhundertfünfunddreißig

1 1
2 5
3 13
4 21
5 37
6 287
7 967
8 1451
9 6257
10 12.327
11 55.699
12 311.422
13 519.612
14 2.744.329
15 5.654.386

Exercise 27.2

Write out the dates in brackets. Remember that when writing the date in figures, Germans add a full stop after the ordinal number.

Example: Heute ist der ___ Januar. (2.) → Heute ist der ***zweite*** Januar.

1 Gestern war der ___ März. (5.)
2 Der ___ April ist ein Montag. (7.)
3 Morgen ist der ___ Mai. (17.)
4 Jans Geburtstag ist der ___ September. (30.)
5 Der Geburtstag von Sybille ist der ___ August. (14.)
6 Der Tag der Arbeit ist der ___ Mai. (1.)
7 Frühlingsanfang ist der ___ März. (21.)
8 Der Tag der Deutschen Einheit ist der ___ Oktober. (3.)
9 Heiligabend ist der ___ Dezember. (24.)

Exercise 27.3

Write down in full when and where these well-known Austrians and Germans were born.

Example: Dürer, Albrecht, *21. Mai 1471 Nürnberg
→ Albrecht Dürer ist am einundzwanzigsten Mai 1471 (vierzehnhunderteinundsiebzig) in Nürnberg geboren.

1 Luther, Martin, *10. November 1483 Eisleben
2 Goethe, Johann Wolfgang von, *28. August 1749 Frankfurt am Main
3 Mozart, Wolfgang Amadeus, *27. Januar 1756 Salzburg
4 Freud, Sigmund, *6. Mai 1856 Freiburg/Mähren
5 Diesel, Rudolf Christian Karl, *18. März 1858 Paris
6 Einstein, Albert, *14. März 1879 Ulm
7 Merkel, Angela, *17. Juli 1954 Hamburg
8 Vettel, Sebastian, *3. Juli 1987 Heppenheim

Exercise 27.4

Translate the following sentences, writing out all numbers.

1 Today is the first of April.
2 Tomorrow is the twenty-third.
3 The sixteenth of June is a Friday.
4 Are you coming at one? (Use the **du** form.)
5 It is one o'clock.
6 She was born on the seventh of January.

7 I am going to Munich on the twenty-eighth of February.
8 The Oktoberfest starts on the twentieth of September.
9 Arnold Schwarzenegger was born on the thirtieth of July 1947 in Austria.
10 She was born in 2012.

Checklist

1 How do you form the cardinal numbers after twenty? What is different from English?
2 What do you need to be aware of when you use **eins**, the number 'one' in German?
3 How do you form ordinal numbers up to 'nineteenth' and from 'twentieth' onwards?
4 What happens to the ending of ordinal numbers when used with **am**?
5 How is English different from German in referring to years?

UNIT 28

Conjunctions and clauses

What are conjunctions?

If you have more than one clause in a sentence, the clauses are usually connected by a linking word. These linking words are 'conjunctions'. They are words such as 'and' **und**, 'or' **oder**, 'but' **aber**, 'because' **weil**:

clause 1	*conjunction*	*clause 2*
He works for TUI,	*and*	she works for BMW.
Er arbeitet bei der TUI	***und***	**sie arbeitet bei BMW.**
He hasn't answered	*because*	he doesn't speak German.
Er hat nicht geantwortet,	***weil***	**er kein Deutsch spricht.**

Conjunctions define relations between clauses

The different conjunctions indicate the relationship between clauses. For instance you can simply link two (or more) clauses by using 'and', or the second clause can give the reason for what is said in the first clause by using 'because'.

In the first sentence, 'and' combines two clauses which are 'equal' and could also stand independently. These types of clauses are called *main clauses*.

In the second sentence, the clause introduced by 'because' is dependent on the main clause and would be meaningless without the main clause. These types of clauses are called *subordinate clauses*.

Two main groups in German

In German, conjunctions are usually divided into two main groups: coordinating and subordinating conjunctions.

Coordinating conjunctions

Coordinating conjunctions include **und** 'and', **aber** 'but' and **oder** 'or', which usually combine two main clauses. They do not affect the word order.

Subordinating conjunctions

Examples of subordinating conjunctions are **dass** 'that' and **weil** 'because'. Conjunctions of this group normally introduce a subordinate clause and send the verb to the end of that clause.

There is no logical reason why certain conjunctions introduce a main clause and others introduce a subordinate clause. You need to learn them by heart. Here are both categories in more detail.

Co-ordinating conjunctions in detail

The most important co-ordinating conjunctions are:

und	and
aber	but
oder	or
denn	because
sondern	but (following a negative)

All these conjunctions work in a similar way to English conjunctions. Their meaning and usage are explained in the following examples.

Coordinating conjunctions in use

Und

Und is used like 'and' in English. It links clauses which could normally stand independently.

Carsten ist Modedesigner *und* Jan ist Online-Redakteur.
Susi kommt aus Deutschland *und* Renée kommt aus Frankreich.

If the subject is the same in the two clauses which are connected by **und**, then you can (but do not need to) repeat it in the second clause:

***Carsten* ist Modedesigner *und er* arbeitet freiberuflich.**	Carsten is a fashion designer, and he works as a freelancer.
***Carsten* ist Modedesigner *und* arbeitet freiberuflich.**	Carsten is a fashion designer and works as a freelancer.

Note that there is normally no comma before **und**.

Aber

Aber is normally used like the English 'but'. The second clause contains information contrasting with the information in the first clause:

Ich möchte gern kommen, *aber* ich habe leider keine Zeit.	I would like to come, but unfortunately I don't have time.
Sie wohnt seit einem Jahr in Madrid, *aber* sie spricht immer noch kein Spanisch.	She has been living in Madrid for a year, but she still doesn't speak any Spanish.

Note that there is always a comma in front of the conjunction **aber**.

Oder

Oder works like the English 'or'. The second clause expresses an alternative:

Möchtest du relaxen *oder* willst du lieber joggen gehen?	Would you like to relax, or would you prefer to go jogging?
Wir können uns eine Pizza machen *oder* möchtest du essen gehen?	We can make a pizza, or would you like to go out to eat?

At this stage, you will most often use **oder** when you are making suggestions or when you are asking questions.

Denn

Denn works like the English 'because'. It introduces a clause which gives a reason for the first clause:

Er kann nicht kommen, *denn* er ist krank.	He can't come because he is ill.
Tina möchte Ingenieurin werden, *denn* sie interessiert sich für Technik.	Tina would like to become an engineer because she's interested in technology.

Note that there is always a comma before the conjunction **denn**.

Sondern

Sondern expresses the idea of 'but' after a negative statement:

Zürich liegt nicht in Österreich, *sondern* in der Schweiz.	Zürich isn't in Austria but in Switzerland.
Ich möchte keine Cola, *sondern* eine Limo.	I don't want a Coke but a lemonade.

Like **denn** and **aber**, **sondern** is preceded by a comma. **Sondern** is used in the sense of 'but . . . instead' after a negative clause, contradicting the negative information.

Subordinating conjunctions

Subordinating conjunctions send the verb to the end

Subordinating conjunctions such as **dass** 'that', **obwohl** 'although' and **weil** 'because' introduce a subordinate clause and send the verb to the end. Here are some examples:

Ich denke, *dass* sie aus den USA *kommen.*	I think that they come from the United States.
Er ging ins Bett, *obwohl* er nicht müde *war.*	He went to bed although he wasn't tired.
Sie shoppt oft online, weil sie sehr busy *ist.*	She often does her shopping online because she is very busy.

The most important subordinating conjunctions in German include:

dass	that
obwohl	although
weil	because
als	when (*referring to past events*)
wenn	if, when, whenever
ob	whether
nachdem	after
während	during

The meaning and usage of the conjunctions you are most likely to use as a beginner are explained in the following examples.

Some subordinating conjunctions in use

Dass

Dass is used like the English 'that' after verbs such as **glauben** 'to believe', **meinen** 'to be of the opinion' and **denken** 'to think' or with reported speech (after, for example, **sagen** 'say' or **berichten** 'report'):

Denkst du, *dass* es morgen schön *wird*?	Do you think that it will be nice tomorrow?
Er sagte, *dass* er leider keine Zeit *hat.*	He said that he didn't have any time, unfortunately.

Obwohl

Obwohl is used to express a qualification, a contrast. The English equivalent is 'although':

Ich habe das Tablet gekauft, *obwohl* es teuer *war.*	I bought the tablet although it was expensive.
Ich muss noch arbeiten, *obwohl* ich keine Lust mehr *habe.*	I've got to do some more work although I don't feel like it.

Weil

Weil is used for the English 'because'. It is similar to **denn**, but is used more frequently. However, the meaning of **denn** and **weil** is exactly the same.

Sie fühlt sich fitter, *weil* sie mehr Sport *macht.*	She feels fitter because she is doing more sport.
Ich konnte nicht anrufen, *weil* das Akku von meinem Smartphone leer *war.*	I couldn't call because the battery of my smartphone was empty.

Als

Als is used when referring to a single event or a longer period in the past:

Ich habe etwas gekocht, *als* ich nach Hause *kam.*	I cooked something when I came home.
Ich lebte in Kanada, *als* ich ein Kind *war.*	I lived in Canada when I was a child.

Wenn

Wenn has two uses. One of them corresponds to the English 'if ':

***Wenn* du Lust *hast*, können wir einen Film sehen.**	If you feel like it, we can watch a film.
Ich helfe dir, *wenn* du dich *anstrengst.*	I'll help you if you make an effort.

The other use refers to events happening on a *regular basis* and corresponds to the English 'whenever'. This can be applied to the present and past:

Er hat nie Zeit, *wenn* seine Freundin da *ist.*	He's never free when his girlfriend is visiting.
Er besuchte mich immer, *wenn* er in Hamburg *war.*	He always visited me when he was in Hamburg.

The easiest way of checking whether you use **wenn** or **als** in the past tense is to consider whether you can use 'whenever' in English. If you can, then you normally use **wenn** in German:

***Wenn* er Zeit *hatte*, ging er ins Theater.**	Whenever he had time he went to the theatre.
***Wenn* ich seine Stimme hörte, *dachte* ich an meinen Bruder.**	Whenever I heard the his voice I thought of my brother.

Use of commas

You probably noticed in the above examples that every subordinating conjunction is preceded by a comma. This is obligatory in written German.

Two verbs in a subordinate clause

If there is more than one verb form in a subordinate clause, the finite verb, the verb which takes the relevant ending and changes its form, moves to the very last position:

Ich mag meinen Job, obwohl ich oft lange arbeiten *muss*.
Er kommt später, weil er eingekauft *hat*.
Ich habe etwas gekocht, als ich nach Hause gekommen *bin*.

Often the verb in the final position is either a modal verb or an auxiliary verb (**haben** or **sein**).

Starting with a subordinate clause

It is also quite common in German to start a sentence with a subordinate clause. In this case the verb of the subordinate clause goes to the end as usual and the verb of the main clause moves to the front of its clause:

Wenn es *regnet*, *bleiben* wir zu Hause.
Weil er sehr busy *ist*, *shoppt* er oft online.
Als ich ein Kind *war*, *spielte* ich viel Fußball.

As you can see the two verbs stand next to each other, separated by a comma.

Conjunctions and clauses – the main points

Here are some points to remember about conjunctions and clauses:

- If you are linking two clauses with **und** and the subject is the same in both of them, you don't need to repeat it in the second clause.
- **Denn** and **weil** both mean 'because'.
- **Wenn** and **als** have slightly different meanings in German, but English does not differentiate and uses only 'when'.
- In a subordinate clause, the verb is always at the end.
- There is always a comma before conjunctions introducing a subordinate clause and before **aber** and **denn**.

Did you know?

Als is a good example of a word that has different meanings and usages in a language. Apart from introducing a clause and referring to the past, meaning 'when', it is used in comparisons as 'than' and can also take on the meaning of 'as (a)':

Er war glücklich, als er das Geschenk sah.
Berlin ist kleiner als London.
Sie arbeitet als Verkäuferin.

Exercise 28.1

Join the following sentences by using **und**, **aber**, **oder**, **sondern** or **denn**.

Example: Basel liegt nicht in Österreich. Es liegt in der Schweiz.
→ Basel liegt nicht in Österreich, ***sondern*** in der Schweiz.

1 Das ist nicht Jude Law. Das ist Benedict Cumberbatch.
2 Sandra kommt später. Sie muss arbeiten.
3 Marcell ist Student. Er jobbt am Wochenende in einem Supermarkt.
4 Möchtest du zu Hause bleiben? Willst du in die Stadt fahren?
5 Caroline wohnt seit sechs Monaten in Berlin. Sie war noch nicht am Brandenburger Tor.
6 Björn will einen Wellnessurlaub machen. Er will relaxen.

Exercise 28.2

Complete the sentences by using one of the following: **dass**, **weil**, **obwohl**, **wenn** or **als**.

1 Er hat nie Zeit, ____ er zu viel arbeitet.
2 Glaubst du, ____ er noch kommt?
3 Pia ist immer glücklich, ____ es Freitag ist.

4 Ich konnte keine SMS schicken, ____ ich keine Netzverbindung hatte.
5 Sie lernt Deutsch, ____ ihre Großeltern aus Hamburg stammen.
6 Wir essen, ____ du fertig bist.
7 Sie gehen joggen, ____ es sehr kalt ist.
8 Er fährt gern nach Paris, ____ er nicht viel Französisch spricht.
9 ____ sie ein Kind war, lebte sie im Ausland.
10 Immer ____ er Geburtstag hatte, gingen sie in den Zoo.
11 Er meint, ____ Deutschland ein interessantes Land ist.
12 Wir können ein paar Clips auf YouTube sehen, ____ du Lust hast.

Exercise 28.3

Link the two sentences by using the conjunction in brackets. Make any necessary changes to the word order.

Example: Wir fahren ans Meer. Es ist schön. (wenn)
→ Wir fahren ans Meer, ***wenn*** es schön ist.

1 Sie macht einen Salat. Sie kommt nach Hause. (wenn)
2 Ich schreibe dir eine SMS. Ich habe Zeit. (wenn)
3 Er macht gern Urlaub in Deutschland. Er mag das Land. (weil)
4 Viele Leute lernen Englisch. Die Sprache ist sehr wichtig. (weil)
5 Sie lebt gern in Berlin. Die Stadt ist oft hektisch und anstrengend. (obwohl)
6 Er fühlt sich oft gestresst. Er macht regelmäßig Yoga. (obwohl)

Now rewrite the sentences, starting with the subordinate clause (**wenn**, **weil**, **obwohl**).

Example: → ***Wenn*** es schön ist, fahren wir ans Meer.

Exercise 28.4

Translate the following sentences into German.

1 He is a designer and works for Google.
2 I don't want coffee but tea.
3 I would like to come, but I have to work.
4 She thinks that it is a good idea.
5 I like Berlin because it is an interesting city.
6 He is learning German because he likes the language.
7 I lived in Canada when I was a child.
8 We stay at home when it's raining.
9 When I have time I'll send you a text message.

Checklist

1 What's the main difference between a main and a subordinate clause?
2 Can you name the five most important coordinating conjunctions which link main clauses?
3 Which conjunctions introduce a subordinate clause?
4 What happens to the verb in a subordinate clause?
5 What is the difference between **wenn** and **als** when referring to events in the past?

UNIT 29
Word order

Word order in English

English has fairly rigid rules about the order of words in a sentence. The basic pattern is the order *subject – verb – object or other elements*.

subject	*verb*	*object or other elements*
Peter	likes	music.
The dog	bites	the man.
We	are going	to Italy next week.

Principles in German

German word order is not as rigid as English word order. However, there are still patterns and rules.

Position of the verb

The most important rules relate to the position of the verb:

- In most German sentences, i.e. in main clauses, the verb has to be in the *second position.*
- If there are two verb forms in a sentence, one moves to the end of the clause (the infinitive or participle), while the other remains the second element.

There are some exceptions to this rule:

- In 'yes or no questions' and the imperative, the verb is in first place.
- In subordinate clauses, the verb or verbs are placed at the end.

Time – manner – place

Another rule refers to the sequencing of various elements in a sentence. Expressions of *time* come before *manner* (how something is done) and *place* (Time – Manner – Place).

Here are all forms in more detail.

The verb in second position

Basic principle

The main rule for word order in German is that in most sentence structures the verb must be in second position:

subject	*verb*	*object or other elements*
Ich	***arbeite***	**bei Google in Berlin.**
Er	***schläft***	**morgens immer sehr lange.**
Wir	***fahren***	**nächste Woche mit Freunden nach Italien.**

This applies to main clauses, which are clauses that can stand independently and have at least a subject and a finite verb. You can see that often the basic pattern in German is just like that in English: *subject – verb – object or other elements*.

Position of other elements

However, some aspects of German word order can be quite flexible. You can put other elements into the first position, for instance a description of time or places.

place or expression of time	*verb*	*subject*	*object or other elements*
In Berlin	***arbeite***	**ich**	**bei Google.**
Morgens	***schläft***	**er**	**immer sehr lange.**
Nächste Woche	***fahren***	**wir**	**mit Freunden nach Italien.**

By doing this, more emphasis can be put on a particular item. Note that while the verb remains in second position, the subject moves behind the verb.

Subject–verb inversion

This feature in German grammar, where the subject is placed directly after the verb when the initial position is taken by another element, is called *subject–verb inversion*. For English speakers it often causes problems, as in English the subject would still precede the verb: 'Next week we'll go to Italy with friends.'

Remember, in German the verb will normally stay in second place and the subject will appear after the verb when, for instance, an expression of time starts the sentence.

Other words which start a sentence

Other words or expressions frequently used as the first element include:

dann	then
danach	afterwards
anschließend	afterwards, subsequently
meistens	usually, mostly
normalerweise	normally
deshalb	that's why, therefore
leider	unfortunately
manchmal	sometimes
zum Glück	fortunately

Remember to apply the *subject–verb inversion* in all these instances:

Dann *trinke ich* einen Tee.	Then I'll have a cup of tea.
Meistens *fahre ich* mit dem Rad.	Usually I go by bike.
Deshalb *konnte ich* nicht kommen.	That's why I couldn't come.
Zum Glück *sprechen sie* Deutsch.	Fortunately they speak German.

Two verbs in a sentence

If you have two verbs in a sentence, one verb form – the verb that takes the relevant ending – goes into the second position, while the other verb form (the infinitive or the past participle) appears at the end. This normally happens with the following structures:

- Modal verbs used with another verb:

Ich *muss* ihm eine SMS *schicken*.	I have to send him a text message.
Hier *darf* man keine Selfies *machen*.	You are not allowed to take selfies here.

- The future tense formed with **werden**:

Was *wirst* du *machen*?	What are you going to do?
Tabea *wird* den Sommer in Australien *verbringen*.	Tabea is going to spend the summer in Australia.

- The present perfect tense:

Sie *hat* mir eine SIM-Karte *gekauft.*	She bought me a SIM card.
Gestern *sind* wir spazieren *gegangen.*	Yesterday we went for a walk.

Separable verbs

Separable verbs follow a similar principle: in a main clause the main part of the verb stays in second position while the prefix goes to the end:

ausdrucken	→ **Er *druckt* die Fotos *aus.***	He is printing out the photos.
aufstehen	→ **Sie *stehen* um acht Uhr *auf.***	They get up at eight o'clock.

Yes or no questions and the imperative

There are two main instances where the verb appears in *first position*:

- *Yes or no questions*:

***Sprechen* Sie Englisch?**	**Do you speak English?**
***Hat* Mira einen Freund?**	**Has Mira got a boyfriend?**

- *The imperative*:

***Gib* mir bitte das I-Pad!**	**Give me the iPad, please!**
***Öffnen* Sie die Tür, bitte.**	**Open the door, please.**

Remember that you don't need structures with 'do' like in English to form *yes or no questions*. Putting the verb in the initial position is sufficient.

Word order in subordinate clauses

The finite verb goes last

In subordinate clauses the rule that the finite verb must be in the second position does not apply. Instead, it goes to the end of the clause. Subordinate clauses are introduced by conjunctions such as **als**, **dass**, **weil**, **wenn** etc.

Ich denke, *dass* sie einen Freund *hat.*	I think that she has a boyfriend.
Ich melde mich, *wenn* ich mehr Zeit *habe.*	I'll contact you when I have more time.

More than one verb in subordinate clauses

If there are two verbs in a subordinate clause, both will move to the end of the clause with the finite verb going into the very last position. This often happens when you are using the *present perfect tense* or a *modal verb*:

Ich bin müde, *weil* ich viel Sport *gemacht habe.*	I am tired because I did a lot of sport.
Er sagt, *dass* er das Handy *reparieren kann.*	He says that he can repair the mobile.

The rule for the order of verbs at the end of the clause is quite simple: place the verb with the verb ending – the finite verb – right at the end of the clause.

Separable verbs

The same principle also applies to separable verbs, which are placed directly in front of the finite verb:

Ich denke, dass er *eingekauft hat.*	I think that he went shopping.

Starting a sentence with a subordinate clause

It is also possible to start a sentence with a subordinate clause. As you would expect, the finite verb of the subordinate clause goes to the end of its clause, but the finite verb in the main clause moves up to the very front of its clause. The two finite verbs are then next to each other, separated by a comma:

Weil ich viel Sport gemacht *habe, bin* ich müde.	Because I did a lot of sport I am tired.
Obwohl sein Vater Deutscher *ist, spricht* er kein Deutsch.	Although his father is German, he doesn't speak German.

Time, manner, place

Basic principles

As you saw earlier, expressions of time or place or another element can quite easily occur in the first position of a sentence if you want to put more emphasis on a particular item.

However, there are a number of guidelines for elements which appear after the verb. Normally they follow the order

- Time (*when?*)
- Manner (*how?*)
- Place (*where/where to?*)

Following the Time – Manner – Place principle, a description of time should come before the other two:

	time (when?)	*manner (how?)*	*place (where/ where to?)*
Ich fahre	**am Wochenende**	**mit dem Bus**	**nach Paris.**
Tom geht	**nach der Arbeit**	**meistens**	**ins Fitnesscenter.**

Other combinations

Often not all three elements are present. However, the order of the remaining items should follow the Time – Manner – Place rule:

	time (when?)	*manner (how?)*	*place (where/where to?)*
Ich fahre		**mit dem Bus**	**nach Paris.**
Tom geht	**nach der Arbeit**		**ins Fitnesscenter.**

Subject–verb inversion

If one of the elements comes in first position, don't forget to apply the subject–verb inversion (the subject comes directly after the finite verb):

Am Wochenende fahre ich mit dem Bus nach Paris.

Did you know?

In this unit you saw many examples in German word order where one verb comes near the beginning of a sentence or clause and the second one appears at the end. In grammar terms, this principle is often called **Satzklammer** 'sentence bracket'. This literally means that the two verb forms 'bracket' the clause.

- For more information on co-ordinating and subordinating conjunctions see Unit 28.

Exercise 29.1

Start these sentences with the word or phrase in italics and make any other necessary changes in the word order.

Example: Sie fahren *in den Ferien* immer nach Italien.
→ In den Ferien fahren sie immer nach Italien.

1 Er fängt seine Arbeit *normalerweise* um acht Uhr an.
2 Jana geht *danach* noch in den Wellnessclub und macht einen Zumbakurs.
3 Ich muss den Termin *leider* canceln.
4 Sie besuchen am Wochenende *meistens* ihre Eltern.
5 Kira hat sich *deshalb* so gefreut.
6 Er hat *zum Glück* noch einen Backup gemacht.

Exercise 29.2

Put the phrases in parentheses into the appropriate position. Remember to follow the Time – Manner – Place rule.

1 Sie gehen in das neue spanische Restaurant. (am Wochenende)
2 Robin fährt morgen zu seinen Eltern. (mit dem Auto)
3 Ich habe gestern Tennis gespielt. (im Park)
4 Ich muss im Supermarkt einkaufen. (noch schnell)
5 Er trifft sich heute Abend mit Freunden. (in der Stadt)
6 Ich bin mit dem Eurostar nach London gefahren. (Weihnachten)

Exercise 29.3

The sentences are all mixed up. Put the words in the correct order. Start with the word in italics.

Examples: ist / gestern / gefahren / *Er* / in den Urlaub
→ Er ist gestern in den Urlaub gefahren.

am Wochenende / besuchen?/ *willst* / du / uns
→ Willst du uns am Wochenende besuchen?

1 Sie / mir / *Können* / helfen?
2 spielen / sehr gut Klavier / kann / *Er*
3 ein Gapjahr / Sebastian / *Nächstes Jahr* / möchte / machen
4 im Januar / die Schule / beenden / wird / *Sie*
5 im Sommer / fahren? / *Wirst* / du / wieder nach Mallorca
6 sein Abitur / *Er* / gemacht / hat / letztes Jahr
7 *Die Kinder* / fern / sehen / den ganzen Tag
8 haben / einen Ausflug / *Gestern* / gemacht / wir / an die See
9 Sie / nicht / dürfen / rauchen / *Hier*
10 schon um fünf Uhr / ist / aufgestanden / *Sie*
11 *Die Leute* / gefreut / haben sich / sehr über unsere Geschenke
12 vor / *Er* / bereitet sich / auf ein wichtiges Meeting
13 bekommen / hat / einen neuen Chef / *Die Lufthansa*
14 in den letzten Jahren / *Die Bevölkerung Berlins* / stark gewachsen / ist
15 haben / wird / weiterhin eine wichtige Rolle / *Deutschland* / in Europa

Exercise 29.4

Translate the following sentences. Use both **du** and **Sie** for 'you'.

1 Usually I get up at seven o'clock.
2 Fortunately, they speak English.
3 He can play football very well.
4 Do you have an iPad?
5 After work, we sometimes go the gym.
6 I think that he works for Oxfam.

7 Although her mother comes from Germany she doesn't speak any German.
8 When I have more time I will spend a year in Austria or Germany.

Checklist

1 What is the position of the finite verb in most sentences in German?
2 What is meant by subject–verb inversion?
3 In what kind of structures is the verb the first element?
4 What is the most important feature in a subordinate clause with regard to word order?
5 Is there a typical order in which you describe where, how or when something happens?

KEY TO EXERCISES AND CHECKLISTS

Unit 1

Checklist

1 You use capital letters at the beginning of sentences and for all nouns. Also the formal 'you' in German (**Sie**) is always spelt with a capital s. 2 You use the letter **ß** after **ei** and **ie** and after **a**, **o** and **u** if these vowels are pronounced long. 3 Umlauts are important because they change the pronunciation and the meaning of words. 4 English gender is biological (persons are masculine or feminine, and things, concepts and ideas are neuter). German gender is grammatical (things can be masculine, feminine or neuter). 5 The position of the verb. 6 No, there is only one tense.

Unit 2

Exercise 2.1

du -st, Sie -en, er/sie/es -t, wir -en, ihr -t, Sie -en, sie -en

Exercise 2.2

1 wohnst, wohne; 2 studierst, studiere; 3 hörst, höre; 4 lernst, lerne; 5 trinkst, trinke; 6 jobbst, jobbe; 7 machst, mache.
Using the Sie form: 1 Wo wohnen Sie? 2 Und was studieren Sie? 3 Welche Musik hören Sie? 4 Welche Sprache lernen Sie im Moment? 5 Was trinken Sie gern? 6 Und jobben Sie? 7 Was machen Sie nicht gern?

Exercise 2.3

1 heiße; 2 Kommst; 3 wohnt; 4 geht; 5 macht; 6 studiert; 7 heißen; 8 heiße; 9 machen; 10 studiere; 11 kommt; 12 macht; 13 wohnt; 14 kommen; 15 gehen; 16 bleiben; 17 lernen; 18 liegt; 19 Versteht; 20 shoppst; 21 Jobbt; 22 jobbt; 23 spielen; 24 joggen, gehen.

Exercise 2.4

1 Ich wohne in Berlin / Ich lebe in Berlin. 2 Er trinkt Kaffee. 3 Sie spielt Tennis. 4 Wir lernen Deutsch. 5 Carla und Sophia spielen Fußball. 6 (*a*) Woher kommst du? (*b*) Woher kommen Sie? 7 (*a*) Wo wohnst du? (*b*) Wo wohnen Sie? (*c*) Wo wohnt ihr? 8 (*a*) Skypst du? (*b*) Skypen Sie?

Checklist

1 The stem is the form of the infinitive without **-en** or **-n**. 2 **-e**, **-st**, **-en**, **-t**. 3 **-en**, **-t**, **-en**, **-en**. 4 There is only one. 5 A finite verb is a verb with 'a' personal ending.

Unit 3

Exercise 3.1

1 ich arbeite, du arbeitest, Sie arbeiten, er/sie/es arbeitet, wir arbeiten, ihr arbeitet, Sie arbeiten, sie arbeiten; 2 ich tanze, du tanzt, Sie tanzen, er/sie/es tanzt, wir tanzen, ihr tanzt, Sie tanzen, sie tanzen; 3 ich heiße, du heißt, Sie heißen, er/sie/es heißt, wir heißen, ihr heißt, Sie heißen, sie heißen; 4 ich reise, du reist, Sie reisen, er/sie/es reist, wir reisen, ihr reist, Sie reisen, sie reisen. 5 ich google, du googelst, Sie googeln, er/sie/es googelt, wir googeln, ihr googelt, Sie googeln, sie googeln.

Exercise 3.2

bleiben	×	helfen	✓	schreiben	×	stehen	×
essen	✓	kommen	×	schwimmen	×	tragen	✓
fahren	✓	nehmen	✓	sehen	✓	treffen	✓
geben	✓	lesen	✓	singen	×	trinken	×
gehen	×	schlafen	✓	sprechen	✓	waschen	✓

Exercise 3.3

1 Er heißt Hans Homann. 2 Er kommt aus Wien. 3 Er arbeitet bei Radio Ö24. 4 Er isst zu Mittag meistens Sushi. 5 Er spricht natürlich Deutsch, aber auch Englisch und Spanisch. 6 Er liest gern Kriminalromane. 7 Er fährt auch gern Ski und schwimmt viel. 8 Er sieht gern Filme mit Michael Keaton. 9 Er schläft oft lange. 10 Er reist gern. 11 Am Abend trifft er oft Freunde im Kaffeehaus. 12 Am Wochenende hilft er manchmal alten Leuten.

Exercise 3.4

1 Sie liest ein Buch. 2 Peter spricht Deutsch und Englisch. 3 Wir sprechen Deutsch und Spanisch. 4 Magda isst gern Pizza. 5 Ich treffe Nadine. 6 Sie nimmt die U-Bahn. 7 Er trägt ein T-Shirt. 8 Es regnet.

Checklist

1 There is an additional **e** before the endings for **du** and **er/sie/es**. 2 These verbs only add **-n** to the stem for the **Sie**, **wir** and plural **sie** forms. Verbs ending in **-eln** also drop the letter **e** when used with **ich**. 3 The **du** and **er/sie/es** forms. 4 **geben**, **helfen**, **treffen**, **essen**, **sprechen**, **nehmen** (**werfen**).

Unit 4

Exercise 4.1

1 Hast; 2 haben; 3 hat; 4 Habt; 5 hat; 6 Haben; 7 habe; 8 haben

Exercise 4.2

1 Sind, bin; 2 Bist; 3 Seid, sind; 4 ist, ist; 5 sind; 6 sind, sind; 7 bist, bin; 8 seid, sind.

Exercise 4.3

1 ich habe, du hast, Sie haben, er/sie/es hat, wir haben, ihr habt, Sie haben, sie haben; 2 ich bin, du bist, Sie sind, er/sie/es ist, wir sind, ihr seid, Sie sind, sie sind.

Exercise 4.4

1 Wir sind aus New York. 2 Sie sind aus Australien. 3 Mario ist aus München. 4 Sind Sie Herr Becker? 5 Er hat eine Schwester. 6 (*a*) Hast du Zeit? (*b*) Haben Sie Zeit? 7 Sie sind Studenten. 8 Ich habe ein Tablet. 9 Es ist schwer. 10 Bonn ist in Deutschland und Salzburg ist in Österreich.

Checklist

1 ich bin, du bist, Sie sind, er/sie/es ist, wir sind, ihr seid, Sie sind, sie sind; 2 **hast** (the form for **du**) and **hat** (the form for **er/sie/es**); 3 Hunger haben, Durst haben, Zeit haben, Langeweile haben, Kopfschmerzen haben; 4 **Sein oder Nichtsein**.

Unit 5

Exercise 5.1

1 steht . . . auf; 2 fängt . . . an; 3 ruft . . . an; 4 druckt . . . aus; 5 hört . . . auf; 6 kauft . . . ein; 7 sieht . . . fern; 8 geht . . . aus; 9 schläft . . . ein. The following verbs require a vowel change: **anfangen**, **fernsehen** and **einschlafen**.

Exercise 5.2

aufstehen	✓	verlieren		abfahren	✓	anrufen	✓
verstehen		fernsehen	✓	anhängen	✓	stattfinden	✓
einladen	✓	mitkommen	✓	bezahlen		erzählen	
aufräumen	✓	frühstücken		einkaufen	✓	benutzen	

Exercise 5.3

1 stehen . . . auf; 2 räumen . . . auf; 3 kauft . . . ein; 4 Kommst . . . mit; 5 findet . . . statt; 6 sieht . . . fern; 7 fährt . . . ab; 8 laden . . . ein; 9 hängt . . . an; 10 ruft . . . an.

Exercise 5.4

1 Ich stehe um sechs Uhr auf. 2 Ich fange meine Arbeit um acht Uhr an. 3 Das Meeting findet am Montag statt. 4 Wann fährt der Zug ab? 5 Wann kommt der Zug an? 6 Die Kinder sehen fern. 7 Kommen Sie/Kommst du mit? 8 Ich hänge die Datei an und drucke den Artikel aus.

Checklist

1 The first part, the prefix. 2 It goes to the very end of a sentence or clause. 3 Separable prefixes include **ab-**, **an-**, **auf-**, **aus-**, **ein-**, **fern-**, **mit-**, **statt-**, **vor-**, **zu-**. 4 In a good conventional dictionary, it should say '*sep*' after the main German entry. 5 Non-separable prefixes include **be-**, **er-**, **ge-** and **ver-**.

Unit 6

Exercise 6.1

1 Bringen; 2 Öffnen; 3 Warten; 4 Schicken; 5 Kommen . . . herein; 6 Fangen . . . an; 7 Seien; 8 Haben.

Exercise 6.2

1 Bring mir noch einen Saft, bitte. 2; Öffne bitte das Fenster. 3 Warte bitte noch fünf Minuten. 4 Schick mir eine SMS. 5 Komm herein! 6 Fang an! 7 Sei bitte ruhig. 8 Hab ein bisschen Geduld.

Exercise 6.3

1 Fahr mehr mit dem Fahrrad. 2 Geh zu einem Yogakurs. 3 Sieh weniger fern. 4 Iss mehr Gemüse. 5 Lies einen Blog über Gesundheit. 6 Schlaf mehr. 7 Sei relaxter. 8 Geh mehr aus. 9 Finde eine bessere Work-Life-Balance.

Exercise 6.4

1 (*a*) Bitte fangen Sie an. (*b*) Bitte fang an. (*c*) Bitte fangt an. 2 (*a*) Öffnen Sie das Fenster. (*b*) Öffne das Fenster. (*c*) Öffnet das Fenster. 3 (*a*) Schicken Sie mir eine SMS. (*b*) Schick mir eine SMS. (*c*) Schickt mir eine SMS. 4 (*a*) Seien Sie vorsichtig. (*b*) Sei vorsichtig. (*c*) Seid vorsichtig.

Checklist

1 There are three: the **du**, **Sie** and **ihr** forms. 2 Use the stem of the verb without an ending. 3 Verbs whose stem ends in **-d**, **-t**, consonant + **m** or consonant + **n** add **-e**. Verbs which have a stem vowel change have the same change in the imperative. However, the stem vowel change **a** to **ä** does not occur in the imperative. 4 The **Sie** comes after the verb.

Unit 7

Exercise 7.1

2 Wo; 3 Wie; 4 Wo (Alternatively: Was); 5 Was; 6 Woher; 7 Wie; 8 Wann; 9 Wie; 10 Woher; 11 Wohin; 12 Wie.

Exercise 7.2

1 Ist das Restaurant wirklich sehr billig? 2 Ist Leon wirklich verheiratet? 3 Macht Frau Weber wirklich viel Sport? 4 Kostet das Smartphone wirklich nur 80 Euro? 5 Stehen Jennifer und Max wirklich um sechs Uhr auf?

Exercise 7.3

1 Wie ist Ihr Name? 2 Was sind Sie von Beruf? 3 Wann beginnt Ihre Arbeit? 4 Ist die Arbeit interessant? 5 Haben Sie Kinder? 6 Sind Sie verheiratet? 7 Was sind Ihre Hobbys? 8 Sprechen Sie Spanisch?

Exercise 7.4

1 Wie ist dein/Ihr Name? 2 Woher kommst du/kommen Sie? 3 Wie ist deine/Ihre E-Mail-Adresse? 4 Wie viel Uhr ist es? 5 Bist du/Sind Sie verheiratet? 6 Hast du/Haben Sie Kinder? 7 Sprichst du/Sprechen Sie Englisch? 8 Was ist er von Beruf?

Checklist

1 **Wie**. 2 At the beginning. 3 After the question word. 4 **Woher** and **wohin**.

Unit 8

Exercise 8.1

1 Die; 2 Die; 3 der; 4 Der; 5 Das; 6 der; 7 das; 8 Der; 9 Die; 10 die.

Exercise 8.2

	definite article	*indefinite article*
masculine	**der**	**ein**
feminine	**die**	**eine**
neuter	**das**	**ein**
plural	**die**	–

Exercise 8.3

1 Der; 2 ein; 3 die; 4 ein, eine; 5 eine; 6 Das.

Exercise 8.4

1 Die Frau kommt aus Berlin. 2 Der Kaffee schmeckt gut. 3 Das Kind ist sieben Jahre alt. 4 Die Kinder spielen Fußball. 5 Er ist Amerikaner. 6 Er ist Lehrer. 7 Dies ist das Brandenburger Tor. 8 Der Frühling war kalt.

Checklist

1 The definite article refers to a person or a thing that is specific or defined, and the indefinite article refers to a noun that is not. 2 **der**, **die**, **das**, **die**. 3 **ein**, **eine**, **ein**. 4 With masculine and feminine countries; for months and seasons; for names of streets and parks; in certain expressions relating to schools and universities; with some abstract nouns. 5 **Dies/Das ist ...** or **Dies sind/Das sind ...** .

Unit 9

Exercise 9.1

1 der; 2 der; 3 das; 4 die; 5 die; 6 der; 7 der; 8 das.

Exercise 9.2

Bäckerei	*f*	Auto	*nt*	Flasche	*f*	Temperatur	*f*
Lampe	*f*	Märchen	*nt*	Metzgerei	*f*	Museum	*nt*
Kirche	*f*	Emigration	*f*	Zentrum	*nt*	Religion	*f*
Liberalismus	*m*	Nation	*f*	Demokratie	*f*	Instrument	*nt*
Zeitung	*f*	Kino	*nt*	Büro	*nt*	Potential	*nt*
Meinung	*f*	Honig	*m*	Universität	*f*	Motor	*m*
Karte	*f*	Optimismus	*m*	Mädchen	*nt*	Natur	*f*

masculine	*feminine*	*neuter*
-ismus; -ig; -or	-e; -ei; -ion; -ie; -tät; -ung; -ur	-al; -ment; -o; -chen; -um

Exercise 9.3

1 *B*erlin ist eine fantastische *S*tadt. 2 *D*as *H*otel liegt sehr zentral. 3 *D*er *S*ervice ist ausgezeichnet und das *E*ssen ist gut. 4 *D*ie *W*oche geht so schnell vorbei. 5 *D*ie *M*enschen in *B*erlin sind sehr freundlich. 6 *H*eute *A*bend gehen wir zuerst in ein *K*onzert und dann in ein *R*estaurant und feiern unseren letzten *T*ag in *B*erlin.

Exercise 9.4

1 Das; 2 Der, das; 3 Die; 4 Die; 5 Die; 6 Die; 7 Das; 8 Das; 9 der; 10 Das, der; 11 Die; 12 Die.

Checklist

1 Masculine: **-er**, **-ig**, **-ismus**, **-ist**, **-ling**, **-or**. Feminine: **-ei**, **-enz**, **-heit**, **-ie**, **-ion**, **-tät**, **-schaft**, **-ung**, **-ur**. Neuter: **-chen**, **-lein**, **-ma**, **-ment**, **-o**, **-um**. 2 Masculine: names of days and months; names of seasons; makes of cars; alcoholic drinks (apart from beer). Feminine: names of motorbikes and ships; names of trees and flowers. Neuter: young persons; names of hotels and cinemas; names of most metals; infinitives used as nouns. 3 The last noun. 4 They are spelt with an initial capital letter.

Unit 10

Exercise 10.1

2 die Mäntel; 3 die Bücher; 4 die Kühlschränke; 5 die Gläser; 6 die Mütter; 7 die Passwörter; 8 die Regale; 9 die Tassen; 10 die Teppiche; 11 die Zeitungen; 12 die Zimmer.

Exercise 10.2

1 Tage; 2 Kurse; 3 Orangensäfte; 4 Gäste; 5 Schnäpse; 6 Tassen; 7 Tomaten; 8 Meinungen; 9 die Städte; 10 Bratwürste; 11 Schiffe; 12 Programme; 13 Häuser; 14 Bücher; 15 Länder; 16 Hotels; 17 Blogs; 18 Handys; 19 Tweets; 20 Sneakers.

Exercise 10.3

masculine	*feminine*	*neuter*
-e; umlaut + **-e**	**-e**; **-en**; umlaut + **-e**	**-e**; umlaut + **-er**

Exercise 10.4

1 Ich möchte zwei Flaschen, bitte. 2 Zwei Bratwürste, bitte. 3 Die Äpfel sind sehr süß. 4 Er hat zwei Schwestern und drei Brüder. 5 Sie liest drei Zeitungen. 6 Das Haus hat vier Zimmer. 7 Die Häuser sind neu. 8 Sie spricht fünf Sprachen. 9 Er hat drei Handys. 10 Die Partys sind immer interessant.

Checklist

1 They add an **-e** and often also an umlaut when the original stem vowel is **a** or **u**. For other changes see pp. 57, 58. 2 They add **-n** or **-en**. For other changes see p. 57. 3 They add **-e** (but no umlaut) or **-er** + umlaut if possible. For other changes see pp. 57, 58. 4 They add **-s**. 5 The plural form is usually given in third place, following the *gender* and the *genitive ending*.

Unit 11

Exercise 11.1

1 <u>Der Mann</u> geht ins Kino. 2 <u>Das Kind</u> spielt mit dem I-Pad. 3 In der Garage steht <u>das Auto</u>. 4 <u>Die Tochter</u> sieht einen Clip auf YouTube. 5 Um acht Uhr verlässt <u>die Nachbarin</u> das Haus. 6 Nach dem Essen trinken <u>die Leute</u> noch Kaffee.

Exercise 11.2

1 Ich schenke *der Frau* (1) (*dative*) *ein Buch* (2) (*accusative*). 2 Er kauft *dem Mädchen* (1) (*dative*) *ein Eis* (2) (*accusative*). 3 Herr Schulz zeigt *dem Gast* (1) (*dative*) *den Garten* (2) (*accusative*). 4 Der Kellner bringt *dem Mann* (1) (*dative*) *das Essen* (2) (*accusative*).

Exercise 11.3

The indefinite article

	accusative		*dative*		*genitive*	
masculine	einen	✓	einem	✓	eines	✓
feminine	eine		einer	✓	einer	✓
neuter	ein		einem	✓	eines	✓

The definite article

	accusative		*dative*		*genitive*	
masculine	den	✓	dem	✓	des	✓
feminine	die		der	✓	der	✓
neuter	das		dem	✓	des	✓

Checklist

1 First, the role the noun plays in a sentence: is it the subject or an object? Second, the verb: does it require the direct object, dative case or genitive case? Third, a preposition, which requires a certain case to follow. 3 The accusative case. 4 The dative case. 5 Words that accompany nouns such as the articles 'the' and 'a'.

Unit 12

Exercise 12.1

1 ein, Der; 2 ein, Das; 3 eine, Die; 4 eine, Die; 5 ein, Das; 6 ein, Der; 7 Die; 8 Die.

Exercise 12.2

1 Morgen fahren wir nach Italien. 2 Meine Mutter heißt Svenja. 3 Hast du heute Zeit? 4 Im Sommer wohnen wir in Berlin. 5 Trinkt er gern Wein? 6 Hier ist die Musik sehr laut. 7 Nächsten Monat gehe ich in ein Konzert.

Exercise 12.3

1 Das ist ein Haus. *or* Dies ist ein Haus. 2 Das Haus ist sehr alt. 3 Der Mann heißt Mario. 4 Die Zeitung ist sehr interessant. 5 Edeka ist ein Supermarkt in Deutschland. 6 Meine Frau arbeitet in Hamburg. 7 Wo sind die Kinder?

Checklist

1 It is the subject of the sentence. 2 You use the nominative after **werden** and after **sein**. 3 You ask the question 'Who or what is doing the action?' 4 Determiner endings: masculine: **der**, **ein**, **mein**, **kein**. Feminine: **die**, **eine**, **meine**, **keine**. Neuter: **das**, **ein**, **mein**, **kein**. Plural: **die**, –, **meine**, **keine**.

Unit 13

Exercise 13.1

1 Ich brauche eine Lampe. 2 Ich brauche eine Blumenvase. 3 Ich brauche einen Küchentisch. 4 Ich brauche ein Sofa. 5 Ich brauche ein Bücherregal. 6 Ich brauche einen Teppich. 7 Ich brauche einen Kühlschrank. 8 Ich brauche eine Mikrowelle. 9 Ich brauche eine Kaffeemaschine. 10 Ich brauche eine Waschmaschine. 11 Ich brauche ein Handy. 12 Ich brauche einen Camcorder.

Exercise 13.2

1 einen; 2 eine; 3 meine; 4 meinen; 5 das; 6 die; 7 den; 8 die.

Exercise 13.3

1 Ich möchte einen Kaffee. 2 Der Mann kauft den Computer. 3 Die Frau kauft den Camcorder. 4 Das Kind liest das Buch. 5 Das Sweatshirt ist für meinen Bruder. 6 Das Buch ist für meine Schwester. 7 Wir gehen durch den Park. 8 Ich brauche eine Kaffeemaschine und eine Mikrowelle. 9 Ich brauche einen Regenschirm. 10 Ich bin für die Idee.

Checklist

1 For the direct object, after verbs taking the accusative case and after prepositions taking the accusative. 2 The masculine endings only. 3 It says '*vt*' after the headword. 4 Prepositions: **bis** 'until', **durch** 'through', **für** 'for', **gegen** 'against', 'around' (for time), **ohne** 'without'.

Unit 14

Exercise 14.1

1 Sie gibt dem Großvater ein Buch über Nelson Mandela. 2 Sie gibt der Mutter einen Strauß Blumen. 3 Sie gibt dem Vater eine Flasche Wein. 4 Sie gibt dem Sohn eine Star-Wars-Tasse. 5 Sie gibt der Tochter ein Haarband. 6 Sie gibt dem Baby einen Ball.

Exercise 14.2

1 dem; 2 dem; 3 der; 4 einem; 5 einer; 6 der; 7 einem; 8 dem; 9 der; 10 dem; 11 den 20 Mitarbeitern; 12 den Kindern.

Exercise 14.3

1 Sie gibt dem Baby ein Buch. 2 Paulina kauft dem Kind ein Eis. 3 Er gibt dem Großvater eine Flasche Wein. 4 Er folgt dem Mann. 5 Das I-Pad gehört dem Fahrer. 6 Peter hilft dem Mädchen. 7 Er gibt den Kindern einen Fußball. 8 Sie kommt aus der Türkei.

Checklist

1 First, it is mainly used for the indirect object in a sentence; second, after certain verbs; and, third, after several prepositions. 2 The endings of the determiners for masculine and neuter nouns are **dem**, **einem**, **meinem**, **keinem**. 3 For the feminine determiners, they are **der**, **einer**, **meiner**, **keiner**. For the plural: **den**, –, **keinen**, **meinen**. 4 Most dative plural noun endings have an **-n** added.

Unit 15

Exercise 15.1

1 Das ist das Mountainbike von meinem Sohn. 2 Das sind die Sportsachen von meiner Frau. 3 Das ist das Spielzeug von meinem Kind. 4 Das ist die Frau von meinem Chef. 5 Da vorne steht der Scooter von meiner Schwester. 6 Die Lehrerin von meinem Englischkurs kommt aus New York. 7 Der Trainer von unserer Hockeymannschaft ist sehr gut. 8 Die Meinung von meinen Freunden ist mir sehr wichtig.

Exercise 15.2

1 mein*es* Sohn*es*; 2 d*es* Buch*es*; 3 d*er* Sängerin; 4 mein*er* Yogalehrerin; 5 mein*er* Chefin; 6 mein*es* neuen Tablet*s* 7 d*es* schlechten Wetter*s*; 8 ihr*er* Mittagspause.

Exercise 15.3

1 Das/Dies ist der Scooter meines Bruders. 2 Das/Dies ist das Auto meiner Schwester. 3 Das/Dies sind die Freunde meiner Tochter. 4 Das/Dies ist Paulas Tasche. 5 Es war Tims Fehler.
Note that for sentences 1, 2, 3 and 4 you can either use **Das** or **Dies**. See page 45.

Checklist

1 The genitive is determined by its role in a sentence, indicating either possession or ownership, and by a number of prepositions which require the genitive case. 2 The endings of masculine and neuter determiners are **des**, **eines**, **keines**, **meines**. 3 The feminine endings are **der**, **einer**, **keiner**, **meiner**. The plural endings are **der**, –, **keiner**, **meiner**. 4 Short nouns add **-es** and longer nouns **-s**.

Unit 16

Exercise 16.1

1 Er; 2 Sie; 3 Es; 4 Sie; 5 Sie; 6 Sie; 7 Sie; 8 Es; 9 Er; 10 Sie.

Exercise 16.2

1 Ja, ich kaufe es. 2 Ja, ich kenne ihn. 3 Ja, ich kenne sie. 4 Ja, ich habe es. 5 Ja, ich trinke ihn. 6 Ja, ich möchte sie. 7 Ja, ich mag sie. 8 Ja, ich besuche dich. 9 Ja, ich besuche euch. 10 Ja, mir geht es gut / Ja, es geht mir gut.

Exercise 16.3

1 ihr; 2 mir; 3 ihm; 4 ihnen; 5 dir; 6 Ihnen; 7 mir; 8 ihnen; 9 uns; 10 euch.

Exercise 16.4

1 Der Kaffee ist gut. Er ist gut. 2 Die Jacke ist neu. Sie ist neu. 3 Ist das für mich? 4 Ich kaufe ihm eine Flasche Wein. 5 Er schickt ihr eine SMS. 6 Wie geht es dir/Ihnen? 7 Es geht mir sehr gut. 8 Es tut mir leid.

Checklist

1 The formal you, **Sie**, is used for people whom you don't know well and who are older than you. You use **du/ihr** for family, friends, children and animals. 2 The German grammatical gender is not always used according to 'biological' gender. Personal pronouns can have different functions in a sentence and therefore can

be in different cases. 3 **mich, dich, Sie, ihn, sie, es, uns, euch, Sie, sie.** 4 **mir, dir, Ihnen, ihm, ihr, ihm, uns, euch, Ihnen, ihnen.** 5 **Wie geht es dir/Ihnen/euch? Es geht mir gut. Es tut mir leid. Meine Nase/Mein Bein tut mir weh. Mir ist kalt/heiß.**

Unit 17

Exercise 17.1

my: **mein**; your (singular, informal): **dein**; your (singular, formal): **Ihr**; his: **sein**; her: **ihr**; its: **sein**; our: **unser**; your (plural, informal): **euer**; your (plural, formal): **Ihr**; their: **ihr**.

Exercise 17.2

1 dein, Mein; 2 deine, Meine; 3 sein, ihr; 4 Ihre, Meine; 5 eure, Unsere; 6 eure, unsere.

Exercise 17.3

1 Tom sucht seine Brille. 2 Paula sucht ihr Geld. 3 Mehmet sucht seinen Controller. 4 Marion sucht ihren Schal. 5 Martha sucht ihre SIM-Karte. 6 Benjamin sucht sein I-Pad. 7 Peter sucht seine Schuhe. 8 Jessica und Pia suchen ihre Pässe.

Exercise 17.4

1 Das/Dies ist mein Vater. 2 Das/dies ist meine Mutter. 3 Marc sucht seine SIM-Karte. 4 Susanne sucht ihren Führerschein. 5 Wir treffen unsere Freunde. 6 Sebastian spricht mit seiner Mutter. 7 Arianne spricht mit ihrem Bruder. 8 Die Kinder sprechen mit ihren Großeltern.

Checklist

1 **mein, dein, Ihr, sein, ihr, sein, unser, euer, Ihr, ihr.** 2 They must agree in gender, number and case with the noun that they are linked to. 3 **Euer.** 4 **Ihr** can refer to 'your', formal, in the singular and in the plural, and **ihr** can either mean 'her' or 'their'.

Unit 18

Exercise 18.1

amüsieren	✓	beeilen	✓	entscheiden	✓	einkaufen	
anziehen	✓	studieren		entschuldigen	✓	tanzen	

ausgehen		duschen	✓	fahren		treffen	✓
ausziehen	✓	arbeiten		kämmen	✓	waschen	✓

Exercise 18.2

1 Er entschuldigt sich bei seiner Freundin. 2 Das Kind kämmt sich nicht gern. 3 Ich ärgere mich über die Preise. 4 Ich ziehe mich um. 5 Anne zieht sich ihr neues Kleid an. 6 Die Kinder waschen sich. 7 Die Spieler duschen sich nach dem Spiel. 8 Wir beeilen uns. 9 Wir treffen uns um acht Uhr. 10 Wir verabschieden uns.

Exercise 18.3

1 mir; 2 dir; 3 dir; 4 mir.

Exercise 18.4

1 Ich dusche mich. 2 Ich putze mir die Zähne. 3 Ich ziehe mich an. 4 Ich kämme mich./Ich kämme mir die Haare. 5 Ich ziehe mir eine Jacke an. 6 Ich beeile mich.

Checklist

1 A reflexive pronoun. 2 Activities from your daily routine such as washing, brushing teeth and dressing. 3 The accusative case. 4 Here are some examples: **Ich wasche mir die Haare. Du wäscht dir die Haare. Wasch dir die Hände! Ich putze mir die Zähne. Er putzt sich die Nase. Sie schminkt sich.**

Unit 19

Exercise 19.1

1 Franziska joggt nicht. 2 Mario ist nicht clever. 3 Der Film ist nicht interessant. 4 Das Wetter in England ist nicht gut. 5 Er fotografiert nicht gern. 6 Nadine macht nicht gern Outdoorsport. 7 Er fährt nicht gern mit seinem Mountainbike. 8 Monica kommt nicht aus Österreich. 9 Er ist nicht verheiratet. 10 Mia studiert nicht Medizin. 11 Sie geht heute nicht ins Konzert. 12 Er spielt nicht gut Klavier. 13 Ich habe die App nicht gekauft. 14 Er hat die E-Mail nicht gelesen.

Exercise 19.2

2 keine; 3 kein; 4 keinen; 5 keine; 6 kein; 7 kein.

Exercise 19.3

1 Nein, das ist kein Park. 2 Nein, das ist keine Kneipe. 3 Nein, ich habe kein Auto. 4 Nein (danke), ich möchte keinen Kaffee. 5 Nein, ich nehme keinen Nachtisch. 6 Nein, Alina hat keine Schwester. 7 Nein, das Hotel hat keinen Wellnessbereich. 8 Nein, ich habe keine Geschwister. 9 Nein, ich habe keine Wanderschuhe. 10 Nein, Freiburg hat keine U-Bahn. 11 Nein, Julian hat kein Geld. 12 Nein, ich habe keine Zeit.

Exercise 19.4

1 Luke arbeitet nicht. 2 Das Hotel ist nicht schön. 3 Das Tablet ist nicht billig. 4 Paul hat kein Mountainbike. 5 Sie haben kein Auto. 6 Das/Dies ist keine gute Idee. 7 Er hat keine Zeit. 8 Sie wohnt nicht in London, sondern in New York. 9 Ich trinke keinen Kaffee, sondern Tee. 10 Das/Dies ist kein Problem.

Checklist

1 **Nicht** is normally used in connection with *adjectives* and *verbs*. 2 **Kein** is normally linked to *nouns*. 3 **Kein** must agree with the noun in gender (*masculine, feminine, neuter*), number (*singular, plural*) and case (*nominative, accusative, dative, genitive*). 4 **sondern**.

Unit 20

Exercise 20.1

	comparative	*superlative*
klein	klein*er*	am klein*sten*
langweilig	langweilig*er*	am langweilig*sten*
alt	ält*er*	am ält*esten*
groß	größ*er*	am grö*ßten*
hoch	höh*er*	am höch*sten*
interessant	interessant*er*	am interessant*esten*
intelligent	intelligent*er*	am intelligent*esten*
umweltfreundlich	umweltfreundlich*er*	am umweltfreundlich*sten*
gut	bess*er*	am be*sten*
gern	lieb*er*	am lieb*sten*
viel	mehr	am mei*sten*

Exercise 20.2

1 länger; 2 flacher; 3 billiger; 4 teurer; 5 interessanter; 6 langweiliger; 7 ruhiger; 8 kälter; 9 ökologischer; 10 gesünder; 11 höchsten; 12 liebsten; 13 umweltfreundlichsten; 14 coolsten; 15 besten.

Exercise 20.3

1 Hamburg ist größer. Berlin ist am größten. 2 Die Elbe ist länger. Der Rhein ist am längsten. 3 Pasta schmeckt besser. Pizza schmeckt am besten. 4 Jan spricht klarer. Anna spricht am klarsten. 5 Nele macht mehr Sport. Anke macht am meisten Sport. 6 Ich trinke lieber grünen Tee. Ich trinke am liebsten schwarzen Tee. 7 Ungarisch ist komplizierter. Chinesisch ist am kompliziertesten. 8 Hamburg ist multikultureller. Berlin ist am multikulturellsten.

Exercise 20.4

1 London ist größer als Paris. 2 Der Rhein ist länger als die Donau. 3 Jan ist älter als Gabriel. 4 Boris ist intelligenter als Moritz. 5 Hannah ist am intelligentesten. 6 Der Zug ist ökologischer als das Flugzeug. 7 Das Buch ist besser als der Film. 8 Tim ist so groß wie sein Bruder. 9 Diese Pizza schmeckt am besten.

Checklist

1 It is formed by adding **-er** to the basic form. 2 When the adjective comes after the noun, you simply add **-sten** to the basic form and use the word **am** beforehand. 3 No. 4 In most monosyllabic adjectives. 5 To make them easier to pronounce, adjectives ending in **-er** and **-el** drop the **e** in the comparative. In the superlative, adjectives ending in **-d**, **-t**, **-s**, **-z** usually add an extra **e** before **–sten**.

Unit 21

Exercise 21.1

	dürfen	*können*	*müssen*	*sollen*	*wollen*	*mögen*
ich	darf	kann	muss	soll	will	mag
du	darfst	kannst	musst	sollst	willst	magst
Sie	dürfen	können	müssen	sollen	wollen	mögen
er/sie/es	darf	kann	muss	soll	will	mag
wir	dürfen	können	müssen	sollen	wollen	mögen
ihr	dürft	könnt	müsst	sollt	wollt	mögt

	dürfen	*können*	*müssen*	*sollen*	*wollen*	*mögen*
Sie	dürfen	können	müssen	sollen	wollen	mögen
sie	dürfen	können	müssen	sollen	wollen	mögen

Exercise 21.2

1 kann; 2 Kannst; 3 kann; 4 Könnt; 5 können; 6 kann.

Exercise 21.3

1 Darf; 2 darf; 3 dürfen; 4 soll; 5 Musst; 6 möchte; 7 will; 8 Wollt; 9 Kann; 10 will; 11 Möchtet; 12 soll; 13 Können; 14 sollst; 15 müssen; 16 Kannst.

Exercise 21.4

1 Ich kann gut kochen. 2 Er will gesünder leben. 3 Sie soll mehr Sport machen. 4 Wir möchten bezahlen. 5 Ich mag Berlin. 6 Ich möchte einen Kaffee, bitte. 7 Kannst du mir helfen?/Können Sie mir helfen? 8 Darf ich dich etwas fragen?/Darf ich Sie etwas fragen? 9 Ich muss einkaufen gehen. 10 Du darfst hier nicht parken./Sie dürfen hier nicht parken.

Checklist

1 There is no verb ending for the **ich** and **er/sie/es** forms. The stem vowel changes for **ich**, **du** and **er/sie/es** except for **sollen**. 2 It goes to the end of the sentence. 3 The separable verb doesn't split apart and goes to the end of the sentence. 4 **Mögen** is used only in connection with nouns. **Gern** is used with verbs. 5 You would translate it as **Er darf nicht**.

Unit 22

Exercise 22.1

arbeiten		hören		nehmen	✓	sprechen	✓
bleiben	✓*	kaufen		schreiben	✓	stehen	✓
essen	✓	kommen	✓*	schwimmen	✓*	treffen	✓
fahren	✓	lesen	✓	sehen	✓	trinken	✓
gehen	✓*	machen		spielen		wohnen	

Exercise 22.2

1 hat, gearbeitet; 2 habe, gehört; 3 hat, gekauft; 4 haben, gesagt; 5 haben, gewartet; 6 hast, gemacht; 7 hat, gepostet; 8 hat, eingekauft; 9 habe, zugemacht; 10 haben, studiert; 11 hat, bezahlt; 12 Hast, gecheckt.

Exercise 22.3

1 Ich habe ein Croissant mit Marmelade gegessen. 2 Ich habe Jasmintee getrunken. 3 Ich habe die Zeitung gelesen. 4 Ich bin mit dem Fahrrad zur Arbeit gefahren. 5 Ich habe E-Mails geschrieben. 6 Ich habe mit Kunden gesprochen. 7 Um halb sieben bin ich gejoggt. 8 Um acht Uhr habe ich einen Freund getroffen. 9 Wir sind in ein Restaurant gegangen. 10 Um elf Uhr bin ich zu Hause gewesen./Um elf Uhr war ich zu Hause. 11 Ich habe einen Clip auf YouTube gesehen. 12 Ich bin um Mitternacht ins Bett gegangen. 13 Ich habe gleich geschlafen.

Exercise 22.4

1 Maya hat bis neun Uhr gearbeitet. 2 Er hat ein T-Shirt gekauft. 3 Martina hat in Berlin studiert. 4 Sie haben online bezahlt. 5 Er ist in ein Restaurant gegangen. 6 Sie haben ferngesehen. 7 Wann bist du aufgestanden?/Wann sind Sie aufgestanden?/Wann seid ihr aufgestanden? 8 Was hast du gestern gemacht?/Was haben Sie gestern gemacht?/Was habt ihr gestern gemacht? 9 Was ist passiert? 10 Er hat ein Foto gepostet.

Checklist

1 It is used mostly for the spoken language, however, in contemporary German it is also increasingly used in less formal writing. 2 With the appropriate form of **haben** and the past participle of the verb. 3 **fahren**, **fliegen**, **gehen**, **kommen**, **schwimmen**, **wachsen**, **reisen**, **joggen**. Also, **bleiben**, **sterben**, **werden**. 4 Regular verbs: **ge** + stem + **t**; irregular verbs: **ge** + stem + **en**. 5 At the end of the sentence.

Unit 23

Exercise 23.1

Nun war das arme Kind in dem großen Wald ganz allein. Da hatte es große Angst. Es wusste nicht, wo es war und fing an zu laufen, bis es bald Abend wurde. Da sah es ein kleines Häuschen und ging hinein. In dem Haus war alles klein: Da stand ein Tisch mit sieben kleinen Tellern. Außerdem gab es sieben Messer und Gabeln und sieben Becher. An der Wand standen sieben Betten. Schneewittchen, weil es so hungrig und durstig war, aß von jedem Teller ein

wenig Gemüse und Brot und trank aus jedem Becher einen Tropfen Wein. Dann, weil es so müde war, legte es sich in ein Bett, aber keins passte; das eine war zu lang, das andere zu kurz, bis endlich das siebente recht war - und darin blieb es liegen, dachte an den lieben Gott und schlief ein.
regular verbs: legte → legen, passte → passte.
irregular verbs: *war* → sein, hatte → haben, fing an → anfangen, wurde → werden, sah → sehen, ging → gehen, stand → stehen, gab → geben, aß → essen, trank → trinken, blieb → bleiben, schlief ein → einschlafen.
mixed verbs: wusste → wissen, dachte → denken.

Exercise 23.2

1 ich spielte, du spieltest, Sie spielten, er/sie/es spielte, wir spielten, ihr spieltet, Sie spielten, sie spielten; 2 ich kaufte, du kauftest, Sie kauften, er/sie/es kaufte, wir kauften, ihr kauftet, Sie kauften, sie kauften; 3 ich wohnte, du wohntest, Sie wohnten, er/sie/es wohnte, wir wohnten, ihr wohntet, Sie wohnten, sie wohnten.

Exercise 23.3

1 blieb; 2 Sahst; 3 gingen; 4 tranken; 5 fuhr; 6 schrieb; 7 wusste; 8 brachte.

Exercise 23.4

1 Gestern spielte ich Tennis. 2 Ich kaufte eine Tasse Kaffee. 3 Als Kind lebte ich in Frankfurt. 4 Ich ging ins Kino. 5 Wir blieben eine Woche. 6 Es war letztes Jahr. 7 Ich stand um acht Uhr auf. 8 Ich wollte kommen, aber ich hatte keine Zeit.

Checklist

1 In written German. 2 You take the stem and add the appropriate endings. 3 They change their stem vowel. 4 **ich –**, **du -st**, **Sie -en**, **er/sie/es –**, **wir -en**, **ihr -t**, **Sie -en**, **sie -en**. 5 **Haben**, **sein** and the modal verbs.

Unit 24

Exercise 24.1

ich werde, du wirst, Sie werden, er/sie/es wird, wir werden, ihr werdet, Sie werden, sie werden.

Exercise 24.2

1 Morgen fahre ich zu meinen Eltern. 2 Bitte rufen Sie in einer halben Stunde wieder an. 3 Nächsten Monat habe ich wieder mehr Zeit. 4 Das Fußballspiel findet am Freitag statt. 5 Wir wollen heute ins Fitnesscenter gehen. 6 Sehen wir uns später? 7 Habt ihr bald Zeit? 8 Wohin fahrt ihr in den Sommerferien?

Exercise 24.3

1 Freya wird ein Buch über Yoga lesen. 2 Jan wird eine Radtour machen. 3 Louis und Anna werden zu Hause bleiben. 4 Ich werde Freunde besuchen. 5 Die Nachbarn werden einen Computerspielabend machen. 6 Valentin wird an seinem Blog schreiben. 7 Annett wird im Supermarkt jobben. 8 Wir werden auf eine Party gehen.

Exercise 24.4

1 (*a*) Ich arbeite am Freitag. (*b*) Ich werde am Freitag arbeiten. 2 (*a*) Ich komme später. (*b*) Ich werde später kommen. 3 (*a*) Er geht morgen ins Kino. (*b*) Er wird morgen ins Kino gehen. 4 (*a*) Am Wochenende bleiben wir zu Hause. (*b*) Am Wochenende werden wir zu Hause bleiben. 5 (*a*) Morgen regnet es. (*b*) Morgen wird es regnen. 6 (*a*) Was machst du später?/Was machen Sie später?/Was macht ihr später? (*b*) Was wirst du später machen?/Was werden Sie später machen?/Was werdet ihr später machen? 7 Was machst du in den Sommerferien?/Was machen Sie in den Sommerferien?/Was macht ihr in den Sommerferien? (*b*) Was wirst du in den Sommerferien machen?/Was werden Sie in den Sommerferien machen?/Was werdet ihr in den Sommerferien machen?

Checklist

1 When there is an expression of time in the sentence that refers to the future. 2 You use a form of **werden** plus the infinitive of the main verb. 3 There is a stem vowel change for the **du** and **er/sie/es** forms; there is no ending for the **er/sie/es** form, and the form for **du** is **wirst** (dropping the **d** at the end of the stem). 4 Its position is at the end of the sentence.

Unit 25

Exercise 25.1

2 bei; 3 nach; 4 mit, zu; 5 in; 6 ins; 7 im; 8 an; 9 um; 10 zum; 11 zur; 12 gegenüber; 13 gegen; 14 für; 15 Während.

Exercise 25.2

only accusative	*only dative*	*accusative or dative*	*genitive*
um für gegen	aus bei nach zu mit gegenüber	in (*ins* when used in the accusative, *im* when used in the dative) an	während

Exercise 25.3

1 den; 2 seine; 3 den; 4 der; 5 dem; 6 einem; 7 zum; 8 der; 9 ins; 10 im; 11 seinen; 12 deinen.

Exercise 25.4

1 Wir gehen durch den Park. 2 Er ist gegen den Plan. 3 Ich fahre mit dem Auto. 4 Marion fährt mit dem Fahrrad. 5 Wie komme ich zum Bahnhof? 6 Wir gehen in ein Restaurant. 7 Gehst du/Gehen Sie ins Kino? 8 Am Wochenende fahre ich nach Berlin.

Checklist

1 *Accusative:* **bis**, **durch**, **für**, **gegen**, **ohne**, **um**. 2 *Dative:* **aus**, **außer**, **bei**, **gegenüber**, **mit**, **nach**, **seit**, **von**, **zu**. 3 The accusative refers to movement; the dative refers to a position. 4 They stand for **auf das**, **bei dem**, **in dem**. Other examples are **durchs**, **fürs**, **ins**, **ums**, **vom**, **zum**, **zur**.

Unit 26

Exercise 26.1

1 schöner; 2 guter; 3 neuen; 4 neue; 5 guten; 6 alten; 7 blauen, coole; 8 neuen; 9 schönsten; 10 besten Freunden.

Exercise 26.2

1 Liebe Susanne; 2 Lieber Daniel; 3 Liebe Eltern; 4 Guten Morgen; 5 Guten Tag; 6 Gute Nacht; 7 Mit freundlichem Gruß; 8 In großer Liebe; 9 Mit vielen Küssen; 10 Mit freundlichen Grüßen.

Exercise 26.3

1 grüne; 2 blaue; 3 weiße; 4 weißen; 5 blaue; 6 blauen; 7 blauen, rote; 8 italienischen.

Exercise 26.4

1 Guten Morgen. 2 Gute Nacht. 3 Es ist ein schöner Tag. 4 Er hat einen neuen Laptop gekauft. 5 Ich mag italienischen Wein. 6 Die rote Jacke ist cool. 7 Ich mag den blauen Anzug. 8 Ich trage die schwarzen Schuhe.

Checklist

1 Adjectives before the noun. 2 *Masculine:* **-er**, **-en**, **-en**, **-en**. *Feminine:* **-e**, **-e**, **-en**, **-en**. *Neuter:* **-es**, **-es**, **-en**, **-en**. *Plural:* **-en**, **-en**, **-en**, **-en**. 3 They function as a 'marker' for the noun. 4 The nominative forms in the singular and the feminine and neuter forms in the accusative.

Unit 27

Exercise 27.1

1 eins; 2 fünf; 3 dreizehn; 4 einundzwanzig; 5 siebenunddreißig; 6 zweihundertsiebenundachtzig; 7 neunhundertsiebenundsechzig; 8 eintausendvierhunderteinundfünfzig; 9 sechstausendzweihundertsiebenundfünfzig; 10 zwölftausenddreihundertsiebenundzwanzig; 11 fünfundfünfzigtausendsechshundertneunundneunzig; 12 dreihundertelftausendvierhundertzweiundzwanzig; 13 fünfhundertneunzehntausendsechshundertzwölf; 14 zwei Millionen siebenhundertvierundvierzigtausenddreihundertneunundzwanzig; 15 fünf Millionen sechshundertvierundfünfzigtausenddreihundertsechsundachtzig.

Exercise 27.2

1 fünfte; 2 siebte; 3 siebzehnte; 4 dreißigste; 5 vierzehnte; 6 erste; 7 einundzwanzigste; 8 dritte; 9 vierundzwanzigste.

Exercise 27.3

1 Martin Luther ist am zehnten November 1483 (vierzehnhundertdreiundachtzig) in Eisleben geboren. 2 Johann Wolfgang von Goethe ist am achtundzwanzigsten August 1749 (siebzehnhundertneunundvierzig) in Frankfurt am Main geboren. 3 Wolfgang Amadeus Mozart ist am siebenundzwanzigsten Januar 1756 (siebzehnhundertsechsundfünfzig) in Salzburg geboren. 4 Sigmund Freud ist am sechsten Mai 1856 (achtzehnhundertsechsundfünfzig) in Freiburg/Mähren geboren. 5 Rudolf Christian Karl Diesel ist am achtzehnten März 1858 (achtzehnhundertachtundfünfzig) in Paris geboren. 6 Albert Einstein ist am vierzehnten März 1879 (achtzehnhundertneunundsiebzig) in Ulm geboren. 7 Angela Merkel ist am siebzehnten Juli 1954 (neunzehnhundertvierundfünfzig) in Hamburg geboren. 8 Sebastian Vettel ist am dritten Juli 1987 (neunzehnhundertsiebenundachtzig) in Heppenheim geboren.

Exercise 27.4

1 Heute ist der erste April. 2 Morgen ist der dreiundzwanzigste. 3 Der sechzehnte Juni ist ein Freitag. 4 Kommst du um eins? 5 Es ist ein Uhr. 6 Sie ist am siebten Januar geboren. 7 Ich fahre am achtundzwanzigsten Februar nach München. 8 Das Oktoberfest beginnt am zwanzigsten September. 9 Arnold Schwarzenegger ist am dreißigsten Juli 1947 (neunzehnhundertsiebenundvierzig) in Österreich geboren. 10 Sie ist 2012 (zweitausendzwölf) geboren.

Checklist

1 You give the single number, then **und** and then the tens. In English, the tens come before the single number. 2 Before a noun, it takes the same endings as the indefinite article **ein**. 3 You add **-te** for numbers up to 19 and **-ste** for numbers from 20 upwards. 4 You normally add **-ten** or **-sten** to the number. 5 You do not use **in** when referring to years in German.

Unit 28

Exercise 28.1

1 Das ist nicht Jude Law, sondern Benedict Cumberbatch. 2 Sandra kommt später, denn sie muss arbeiten. 3 Marcell ist Student und (er) jobbt am Wochenende in einem Supermarkt. 4 Möchtest du zu Hause bleiben oder willst du in die Stadt fahren? 5 Caroline wohnt seit sechs Monaten in Berlin, aber sie war noch nicht am Brandenburger Tor. 6 Björn will einen Wellnessurlaub machen, denn er will relaxen.

Exercise 28.2

1 weil; 2 dass; 3 wenn; 4 weil; 5 weil; 6 wenn; 7 obwohl; 8 obwohl; 9 Als; 10 wenn; 11 dass; 12 wenn.

Exercise 28.3

1 Sie macht einen Salat, wenn sie nach Hause kommt. 2 Ich schreibe dir eine SMS, wenn ich Zeit habe. 3 Er macht gern Urlaub in Deutschland, weil er das Land mag. 4 Viele Leute lernen Englisch, weil die Sprache sehr wichtig ist. 5 Sie lebt gern in Berlin, obwohl die Stadt oft hektisch und anstrengend ist. 6 Er fühlt sich oft gestresst, obwohl er regelmäßig Yoga macht.
Starting with the subordinate clause:

1 Wenn sie nach Hause kommt, macht sie einen Salat. 2 Wenn ich Zeit habe, schreibe ich dir eine SMS. 3 Weil er das Land mag, macht er gern Urlaub in Deutschland. 4 Weil die Sprache sehr wichtig ist, lernen viele Leute

Englisch. 5 Obwohl die Stadt oft hektisch und anstrengend ist, lebt sie gern in Berlin. 6 Obwohl er regelmäßig Yoga macht, fühlt er sich oft gestresst.

Exercise 28.4

1 Er ist Designer und arbeitet bei Google. 2 Ich möchte keinen Kaffee, sondern Tee. 3 Ich möchte kommen, aber ich muss arbeiten. 4 Sie denkt, dass es eine gute Idee ist. 5 Ich mag Berlin, weil es eine interessante Stadt ist. 6 Er lernt Deutsch, weil er die Sprache mag. 7 Ich lebte in Kanada, als ich ein Kind war. 8 Wir bleiben zu Hause, wenn es regnet. 9 Wenn ich Zeit habe, schicke ich dir eine SMS / Wenn ich Zeit habe, werde ich dir eine SMS schicken.

Checklist

1 A main clause can stand independently, but a subordinate clause is dependent on the main clause and can't stand on its own. 2 **und**, **aber**, **oder**, **denn**, **sondern**. 3 They include **dass**, **obwohl**, **weil**, **als**, **wenn**, **ob**, **nachdem** and **während**. 4 It goes to the very end of its clause. 5 **Wenn** refers to events that happen on a regular basis, while **als** refers to a single event or a longer period of time.

Unit 29

Exercise 29.1

1 Normalerweise fängt er seine Arbeit um acht Uhr an. 2 Danach geht Jana noch in den Wellnessclub und macht einen Zumbakurs. 3 Leider muss ich den Termin canceln. 4 Meistens besuchen sie am Wochenende ihre Eltern. 5 Deshalb hat sich Kira so gefreut. 6 Zum Glück hat er noch einen Backup gemacht.

Exercise 29.2

1 Sie gehen am Wochenende in das neue spanische Restaurant. 2 Robert fährt am Wochenende mit dem Auto zu seinen Eltern. 3 Ich habe gestern im Park Tennis gespielt. 4 Ich muss noch schnell im Supermarkt einkaufen. 5 Er trifft sich heute Abend mit Freunden in der Stadt. 6 Ich bin Weihnachten mit dem Eurostar nach London gefahren.

Exercise 29.3

1 Können Sie mir helfen? 2 Er kann sehr gut Klavier spielen. 3 Nächstes Jahr möchte Sebastian ein Gapjahr machen. 4 Sie wird im Januar die Schule beenden. 5 Wirst du im Sommer wieder nach Mallorca fahren? 6 Er hat letztes Jahr sein Abitur gemacht. 7 Die Kinder sehen den ganzen Tag fern.

8 Gestern haben wir einen Ausflug an die See gemacht. 9 Hier dürfen Sie nicht rauchen. 10 Sie ist schon um fünf Uhr aufgestanden. 11 Die Leute haben sich sehr über unsere Geschenke gefreut. 12 Er bereitet sich auf ein wichtiges Meeting vor. 13 Die Lufthansa hat einen neuen Chef bekommen. 14 Die Bevölkerung Berlins ist in den letzten Jahren stark gewachsen. 15 Deutschland wird weiterhin eine wichtige Rolle in Europa haben.

Exercise 29.4

1 Meistens stehe ich um sieben Uhr auf. 2 Zum Glück sprechen sie Englisch. 3 Er kann sehr gut Fußball spielen. 4 Hast du/haben Sie ein I-Pad? 5 Nach der Arbeit gehen wir manchmal ins Fitnesscenter. 6 Ich denke, dass er für Oxfam arbeitet. 7 Obwohl ihre Mutter aus Deutschland kommt, spricht sie kein Deutsch. 8 Wenn ich mehr Zeit habe, verbringe ich ein Jahr in Österreich oder Deutschland./Wenn ich mehr Zeit habe, werde ich ein Jahr in Österreich oder Deutschland verbringen.

Checklist

1 The second position. 2 If a sentence starts with anything other than the subject, then the subject goes directly behind the verb (which is in the second position). 3 In yes or no questions and the imperative. 4 The finite verb is in the last position. 5 Yes, the sequence is time, manner, place.

GLOSSARY OF GRAMMATICAL TERMS

adjectives Words that provide more information about a noun: 'The computer is *new*.' 'The exhibition is *interesting*.' 'It is a *boring* book.'

adverbs Words that provide more information about a verb: 'She sings *beautifully*.' 'The child plays *happily*.'

articles Words that tell you whether a noun is *definite* ('the ball') or *indefinite* ('a ball').

auxiliary verbs Verbs such as **haben** or **sein** which are used to form tenses.

cases The case signals what function a noun plays in a sentence. Cases are also determined by certain verbs and by prepositions. There are four cases in German: *nominative*, *accusative*, *dative* and *genitive*.

clauses Units of words which contain at least a subject and a finite verb: 'I go.' 'They work.' There are two types: *main clauses* and *subordinate clauses*. Any sentence must contain at least one main clause. A sentence can be made up of several clauses.

comparative Form of an adjective or adverb used to describe something that is more or less than another: 'bigger', 'smaller'.

compound nouns Nouns made up of more than one word. Combinations can be, for example, noun + noun (**Bierflasche** 'beer bottle') or adjective + noun (**Großstadt** 'city').

conjunctions Words that link clauses: 'and', 'but', 'because' etc.

determiners General term to describe all words which are closely linked to nouns such as 'a', 'the' and 'my'.

demonstrative A word that indicates or singles out a specific item you refer to, such as 'this'/'that'.

finite verbs Forms of the verb with the personal ending linked to the subject: **ich *gehe*, der Mann *arbeitet*.**

future tense Verb form used to refer to events in the future.

gender Gender indicates whether a noun is *masculine*, *feminine* or *neuter*. In German, gender is grammatical; objects can be masculine or feminine as well as neuter: **der Hut** 'the hat' (masculine), **die Sonne** 'the sun' (feminine). Persons can be neuter: **das Kind** 'the child' (neuter).

imperatives Verb forms used for instructions or orders: '*Open* the window, please!'

indirect object Object indirectly linked to verbs. In English, it is often introduced by 'to' or 'for': 'I said this to John.'

infinitives Basic verb form as listed in the dictionary.

inseparable verbs Verbs with an inseparable prefix such as **be-**, **ver-** or **ent-**. The prefix does not split off from the finite verb. See also **separable verbs**.

intransitive verbs Verbs that do not take a direct object. They are often verbs of motion or a change of state: 'arrive', 'leave'. In German, intransitive verbs form the present perfect tense with **sein**.

modal verbs Verbs that modify an action, such as 'must', 'can' and 'may'.

negatives Words used to negate a sentence or an idea. In German, there are two ways of doing this: **nicht** (with verbs and adjectives) and **kein** (with nouns).

nouns Words for persons, concepts or things. All nouns in German are spelt with an initial capital letter.

object Part of the sentence referring to the receiver or target of the action, e.g. 'the ball' in the sentence 'I kick the ball'.

past participle One of the principal forms of the verb. It is used to form tenses such as the present perfect tense. In English, the past participle of 'to go' is 'gone'; in German, the infinitive is **gehen**, and the past participle is **gegangen**. In English, the past participle of 'to work' is 'worked'; in German, the infinitive is **arbeiten**, and the past participle is **gearbeitet**.

plural Nouns can be one (singular) or more than one (plural).

possessives Words that provide information about relationships between things or people or ideas – what or who 'belongs' to what or whom: 'This is *my* hat.' 'This is *her* car.'

prefixes Prefixes are attached to the beginning of a word. In German, prefixes attached to verbs can be separable, such as **auf-** in **aufstehen** 'to get up' (they are split off from the finite verb), or inseparable, like **ver-** in **verzeihen** 'to forgive' (they remain fixed to the verb). See also **separable verbs** and **inseparable verbs**.

prepositions Words providing information about relationships in space, time or manner: 'under', 'during', 'by' etc.

present perfect tense Tense referring to past events. In English, these events have some link with the present. In German, the present perfect is normally used in the spoken language.

present tense Tense referring to events in the present. In English, there are two forms: 'I am going' and 'I go'. In German, there is only one form: **ich gehe**.

pronouns Words that can stand in for a noun, another pronoun or a noun phrase: 'The man is tall. *He* is tall.' 'That car is beautiful. *It* is beautiful.'

reflexive verbs Verbs that take a pronoun referring back to the subject: 'I hurt myself.' In German, many verbs which refer to daily activities such as washing, combing one's hair etc. are reflexive.

separable verbs Verbs with a prefix such as **auf-**, **unter-** or **mit-** which is split off from the finite verb and goes to the end of the clause: **aufstehen** → **Er** ***steht*** **um fünf Uhr** ***auf.*** See also **inseparable verbs**.

simple past tense Tense indicating that an action takes place in the past. In English, it is used to refer to an action completed in the past: 'She *studied* in Berlin.' In German, it is used in writing and when telling a story or recounting an event.

singular Nouns can be one (singular) or more than one (plural).
stem The part of the verb without an ending. The stem of the verb is given by taking away **-en** from the infinitive: **geh** is the stem of the verb **gehen**.
subject The part of the sentence which is the 'agent' of what is happening: '*The dog* bites the postman.'
tenses Forms of the verb indicating whether the action is taking place in the present, past or future.
transitive verbs Verbs that can take a direct object: 'I buy a hat.' In German, transitive verbs form the present perfect tense with **haben**.
umlaut Symbol found over the letters **ä**, **ö**, **ü**.
verbs Words describing 'actions' and states, such as 'to work' and 'to be'.

COMMON IRREGULAR VERBS

Here is a list of the most commonly used irregular verbs.

- The first two columns give the infinitive, which is the form listed in a dictionary, and the English translation.
- The third column gives the finite form in the present tense only for those verbs which have an irregularity, i.e. verbs with a vowel change and/or other spelling variations.
- The fourth column gives the finite form of the simple past tense.
- The last column gives the past participle form. Verbs that form the present perfect tense with **sein** are indicated by an asterisk.
- All separable verbs are shown with their prefix split off from the verb form in columns three and four.

infinitive		*present tense – irregularities for* **du** *and* **er/sie/es**	*simple past tense for* **ich** *and* **er/sie/es**	*past participle*
anfangen	to start, begin	**fängst an, fängt an**	**fing an**	**angefangen**
anrufen	to call up		**rief an**	**angerufen**
aufstehen	to get up		**stand auf**	**aufgestanden***
beginnen	to begin		**begann**	**begonnen**
bleiben	to stay		**blieb**	**geblieben***
bringen	to bring		**brachte**	**gebracht**
denken	to think		**dachte**	**gedacht**
einladen	to invite	**lädst ein, lädt ein**	**lud ein**	**eingeladen**
empfehlen	to recommend	**empfiehlst, empfiehlt**	**empfahl**	**empfohlen**
essen	to eat	**isst, isst**	**aß**	**gegessen**
fahren	to go (by vehicle)	**fährst, fährt**	**fuhr**	**gefahren***
fallen	to fall	**fällt, fällst**	**fiel**	**gefallen**
finden	to find		**fand**	**gefunden**
fliegen	to fly		**flog**	**geflogen***
geben	to give	**gibst, gibt**	**gab**	**gegeben**

infinitive		*present tense – irregularities for* **du** *and* **er/sie/es**	*simple past tense for* **ich** *and* **er/sie/es**	*past participle*
gefallen	to be pleasing	**gefällst, gefällt**	**gefiel**	**gefallen**
gehen	to go		**ging**	**gegangen***
haben	to have	**hast, hat**	**hatte**	**gehabt**
halten	to hold; to stop	**hältst, hält**	**hielt**	**gehalten**
heißen	to be called	**heißt, heißt**	**hieß**	**geheißen**
helfen	to help	**hilfst, hilft**	**half**	**geholfen**
kennen	to know; to be acquainted with		**kannte**	**gekannt**
kommen	to come		**kam**	**gekommen***
lesen	to read	**liest, liest**	**las**	**gelesen**
nehmen	to take	**nimmst, nimmt**	**nahm**	**genommen**
raten	to advise; to guess	**rätst, rät**	**riet**	**geraten**
schlafen	to sleep	**schläfst, schläft**	**schlief**	**geschlafen**
schreiben	to write		**schrieb**	**geschrieben**
schwimmen	to swim		**schwamm**	**geschwommen***
sehen	to see	**siehst, sieht**	**sah**	**gesehen**
sein	to be	**bist, ist**	**war**	**gewesen***
singen	to sing		**sang**	**gesungen**
sitzen	to sit		**saß**	**gesessen**
sprechen	to speak	**sprichst, spricht**	**sprach**	**gesprochen**
stehen	to stand		**stand**	**gestanden**
tragen	to carry; to wear	**trägst, trägt**	**trug**	**getragen**
treffen	to meet	**triffst, trifft**	**traf**	**getroffen**
trinken	to drink		**trank**	**getrunken**
tun	to do		**tat**	**getan**
umsteigen	to change		**stieg um**	**umgestiegen***
verbinden	to connect		**verband**	**verbunden**
verbringen	to spend		**verbrachte**	**verbracht**
vergessen	to forget	**vergisst, vergisst**	**vergaß**	**vergessen**
verlassen	to leave	**verlässt, verlässt**	**verließ**	**verlassen**
verlieren	to lose		**verlor**	**verloren**
verstehen	to understand		**verstand**	**verstanden**
wachsen	to grow	**wächst, wächst**	**wuchs**	**gewachsen***
waschen	to wash	**wäschst, wäscht**	**wusch**	**gewaschen**
werden	to become	**wirst, wird**	**wurde**	**geworden***
wissen	to know (a fact)	**weißt, weiß**	**wusste**	**gewusst**
ziehen	to pull		**zog**	**gezogen**

INDEX

German words appear in bold. Page numbers in bold refer to the most important text in relation to the entry.